# CHIRICAHUA
# NATIONAL MONUMENT

WRITTEN BY
JANICE EMILY BOWERS

PHOTOGRAPHY BY
GEORGE H.H. HUEY

PUBLISHED BY
SOUTHWEST PARKS AND MONUMENTS ASSOCIATION
TUCSON

Thanks to Chuck Milliken for information about Chiricahua National Monument and comments on the manuscript; and to Steven McLaughlin for critical review of the manuscript, companionship in the field, and most of all, continual encouragement and support.

To the memory of Paul Fugate, a good friend and a ranger at Chiricahua National Monument from 1970 to 1980.

Editorial: T.J. Priehs
Copy editing: Carolyn Dodson
Photography: George H.H. Huey
Design: Lawrence Ormsby and Carole Thickstun

Library of Congress: 88-062022
ISBN: 0-911408-79-7

# CONTENTS

PRELUDE

# VISITORS AND RESIDENTS

Some visitors come to Chiricahua National Monument to see rare birds—the sulphur-bellied flycatcher, the Mexican chickadee, or the blue-throated hummingbird. Others want to escape the summer heat of the surrounding desert. Hikers come to stride across the ridges and into the canyons. Families drive up from the border town of Douglas for Sunday picnics in the campground. Biologists come to study the red-bellied Apache fox squirrel or the long-snouted coatimundi. Some visitors hope to participate vicariously in the Old West, the days of ranching, Apache Indian wars, and military encampments. Others appear out of simple curiosity: what is Chiricahua National Monument all about? For whatever reason, 65,000 people stop by this out-of-the-way corner of Arizona every year.

Visitors quickly learn that Chiricahua National Monument is an intimate place. The drive from the visitor center through the park to the end of the road at Massai Point takes no more than half an hour. An average hiker could easily walk one of the trails in a day with time left over to explore Silver Spur Meadow and visit Faraway Ranch. Because the monument is small—just 12,000 acres—the temptation is to pay it a flying visit of a few hours or a day, then travel onward. "Been there, done that," we say, checking Chiricahua National Monument off our list.

But the visitors who choose to stay a bit longer, or who can return at different seasons, find themselves abundantly rewarded for their efforts. Armed with binoculars, field guides, hand lenses, cameras, notebooks, or sketch pads, they experience the monument first-hand. They try to discern the eighteen layers of volcanic rock exposed in the cliffs and slopes or observe some of the 169 species of birds known in the monument. They identify the wildflowers that grow along the trails or find each of the thirteen species of oaks and pines on the wooded slopes. They sit quietly on fallen logs to watch the antics of gray-breasted jays and Apache fox squirrels. As they hike, they listen to the melodious conversation of a black-headed grosbeak. Quietly, they stalk a mule deer, capturing its image on film just before it breaks for cover. However they spend their days here, they realize that to know even a small place like Chiricahua National Monument requires time, for time reveals the changes and cycles that characterize life.

## CHANGE IS ALL AROUND

Visitors who approach the monument from the west drive through peaceful grassland. From the sagging barb-wire fences that line the road, meadowlarks warble their piercing refrains. The notes float through the open windows of the occasional car or truck as it drives by. Horned larks fly up from the roadway as tires approach, scattering like a handful of gravel flung into the air. Behind the fences, cattle standing in the pastures, their legs hidden in the straw of last summer's grasses, seem to have levitated a foot or two above the ground. Placid and unastonished, they graze unmindful of passing vehicles. Thistles and prickly poppies sprig the roadsides. Not too far away, a green line across the plain traces the course of a streambed, dry much of the year, but lush nonetheless with oaks, walnuts, ashes, and sycamores. In the distance the horizon ends at the Chiricahua Mountains, an indigo blue mass smoky in the haze of morning light.

The scene could have been just like this for the past fifty years or more; only the passing cars and trucks will have changed. It seems that soaptree yucca must have always bloomed in June, its candelabras of white flowers rising erect into the sky or bending all the way to the ground under their own weight. Cicadas must have always shrilled from the hardwood groves in the bottom-lands, and spiraling turkey vultures must have always built their air towers above the golden plain. But this stability is more apparent than real. The signs and portents of change surround us here if we know how to read them.

Soon after entering Chiricahua National Monument, we see one of these signs. A small graveyard by the side of the road, partly shaded by junipers, overgrown with wildflowers and weeds, and encircled by a wrought-iron fence, reminds us that every living thing will undergo the mysterious change from life to death. Another sign of change lies along a nearby creek where scattered bottles, cartridge casings, tin cans, nails, barrel hoops, buttons, and buckles remind us of an encampment of soldiers who departed one hundred years ago, leaving only these fragmentary signs of their occupation.

Not too far away, an old ranch house stands in a field. Unoccupied now, the rooms once rang to the sound of footsteps across the wooden floors. The fireplace once exhaled the fragrant incense of juniper wood, and the fruit trees once provided a bounty of peaches, quinces, and plums for pies and cobblers and for eating out of hand on hot summer days.

These changes—the graveyard, the military encampment, the ranch house—have become part of the human history of the monument, a history intimately connected to a second kind of history, to the turn of seasons and the comings and goings of wild creatures.

Change is all around us at Chiricahua National Monument: in the springtime leafing of the sycamores after they have stood bare-branched all winter; in the arrival of the sulphur-bellied flycatchers in summer and their departure in the fall; in the sudden greening of the grassy hillslopes after summer rains; in the rapid metamorphosis of tadpoles to frogs in streambed pools; in the slow decay of oak leaves, pine needles, and twigs on the forest floor. Change comes as the blue-throated hummingbird arrives in summer, bringing a breath of the tropics, and departs in the fall, taking the scents of juniper and pine steeping in the summer sunshine. Change comes as golden eagles number fewer and fewer over the decades and as shrubs and mesquite trees invade the grassland. Change comes as a kingsnake, grown too large for its skin, rubs between two rocks to pull the old skin off. Change comes as autumn temperatures make nights chilly and every living thing prepares for winter. Even the gray and tan cliffs preserve evidence of change to those who know how to read it, change on a scale we can hardly imagine.

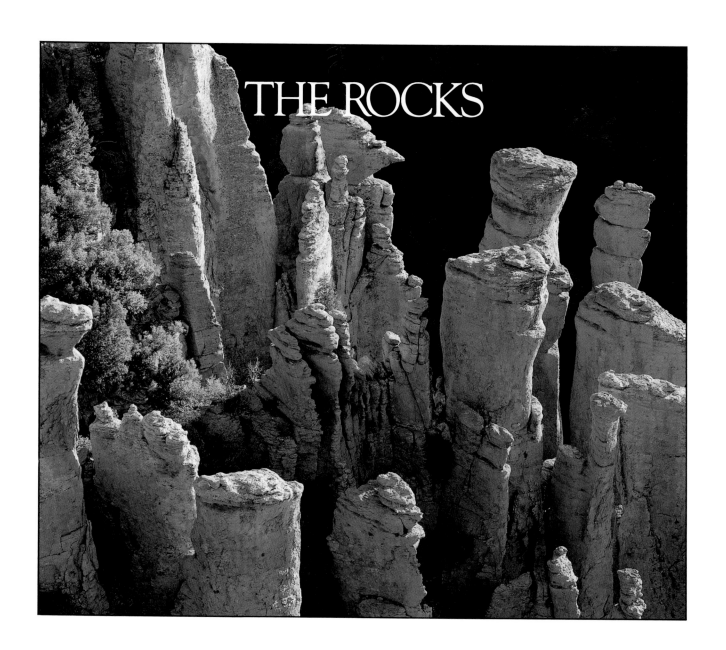

THE ROCKS

CHIRICAHUA NATIONAL MONUMENT

# GLOWING CLOUDS AND BLAZING SANDS

From the road that winds up Bonita Canyon, I admire at a distance a wilderness of rocks—an architectural hodgepodge of spires, pinnacles, columns, battlements, and towers. In some places, the rocks seem almost human, a huge congregation of silent watchers arrayed on the hillslopes. Elsewhere they look like Easter Island figures, brooding and forbidding faces that stare sightlessly out to the valley below, waiting for something or someone that never arrives. Chiricahua National Monument was established in 1924 to preserve these rock formations on the northwestern flank of the Chiricahua Mountains.

Not content with this distant view, I hike into the Heart of Rocks. Here erosion has whittled the rocks into chess pieces—pawns and castles, knights and bishops, kings and queens, all crowded together at one end of the chessboard. As I walk along the trail, I crane my neck to take in the rock columns that tower hundreds of feet above me. Boulder piles converge overhead, forming city-like corridors. Archways span rivers of rock. Bulging pillars side by side make keyholes through which I can peer at the canyons below or the cloud-speckled sky above. Sidling between columns only inches apart, peering down rock chutes into shadowy, waterless wells, I take in a million years of earth history.

No matter where I stand, in a parking lot at Massai Point or in the Heart of Rocks, the landscape waits around me with interminable patience. If I stood here for ninety years, my skin would furrow, my vision would cloud, my hearing would dim, my hair would whiten. While I changed with fearful rapidity, the landscape around me would hardly change at all. I might see some grains of sand and gravel slide down a cliff or a layer of rock slough off a boulder. Perhaps a balanced rock would tumble, echoing loudly between the canyon walls. On a human time scale, the rocks seem static, impervious to time. But this immutability is an illusion.

Twenty-five million years ago this peaceful landscape was the scene of a holocaust as the earth extruded molten rock, clouds of burning, hot ash darkened the sky, and steam and poisonous vapors billowed into the air.

The source of this violent activity was a volcanic caldera some ten miles to the south centered in what is now Turkey Creek, a stream that drains the western flank of the Chiricahua Mountains. Remnants of this caldera (the Spanish word for cauldron) can be seen as outcropping cliffs here and there along the canyon walls in Fife and Pinery canyons. It takes a good imagination to envision the Turkey Creek caldera as it once was. Geologists estimate that it covered a huge, roughly circular area some thirteen miles in diameter.

Eruptions from the Turkey Creek caldera were of a type known to geologists as *nuée ardentes*—French for glowing clouds. As clouds of superheated gases exploded from vents in the caldera floor, they carried a load of incandescent ash and volcanic sand. The heavier sand particles coursed across the ground like a burning avalanche, flowing around obstacles and accumulating in depressions, while the lighter gas and ash particles billowed overhead, hiding the hot-sand avalanche beneath.

These eruptions must have been magnificent, terrifying, awesome events. Again and again, eight or nine times in all, the Turkey Creek caldera spewed forth its glowing clouds of ash and burning avalanches of sand. Over a million years, the caldera disgorged enough material to bury 700 square miles of the surrounding countryside. In the process, the caldera accumulated walls several thousands of feet thick, much of which has since eroded away. (So thoroughly has the crater been erased, it wasn't until the late 1960s that geologists finally pinpointed Turkey Creek as the source of much of the volcanic activity in the area.)

As the red-hot slurry of sand exploded from the Turkey Creek caldera, it flowed so rapidly across the landscape there was little time for it to cool. Once movement had stopped, the molten rock remained hot—probably 650 to 700 degrees centigrade—for some time. This heat was sufficient to weld the loosely clumped particles of ash and sand into the solid rock classified as welded rhyolite tuff.

The cooling process created three different zones within each layer of welded rhyolite tuff. In the lowest zone, the zone of dense welding, the glassy fragments in the magma melted completely together, creating a solid mass free of air space. This zone rings when struck with a hammer. Above the zone of dense welding lies the zone of partial welding. Here heat and pressure were not quite as great, so the different materials in the magma were less completely fused. At the top of each layer, in the zone of no welding, many of the original materials are still discernible, since they have been little altered by heat or pressure.

Each eruption produced a unique layer of welded tuff as characteristic as a fingerprint. The various layers, stacked one above another like layers on a cake, differ in thickness, color, texture, mineral composition, and degree of welding. Nine different rock layers, also called members, originated in the Turkey Creek caldera. Taken together, these layers comprise the Rhyolite Canyon Formation. Its most prominent member, number six, is 880 feet thick. This is the light gray to brownish gray rock of the spires and pinnacles that dominate the landscape at Chiricahua National Monument.

# BEFORE THE CALDERA

In starting the geologic story of Chiricahua National Monument with the eruptions of Turkey Creek caldera, we skipped to the middle of the tale. What did the landscape look like before the Turkey Creek caldera spewed magma over the surrounding countryside? Where does the Chiricahua story actually begin?

It's hard to say. Reading geology from the landscape is like reading a murder mystery, with this difference: mystery readers expect that the author will have planted enough clues for them to guess the murderer, but geologists realize that many vital clues to the history of the landscape were destroyed long ago. Even the hardest rocks crumble into fragments with the continual onslaught of rain and frost and the gnawings of lichens and roots. Running water and wind take the fragments away, and in several million years, an entire mountain can be leveled. Often, as at Chiricahua National Monument, erosion has torn several chapters out of the beginning of the book.

Some of the oldest exposed rocks in the monument are limestones that formed about 120 million years ago. Because limestones are laid down in marine environments, geologists deduce that a shallow inland sea once inundated most of the region. This sea advanced and retreated across southern Arizona for about 450 million years. After its last advance about seventy million years ago, the sea disappeared forever.

A period of nearly forty million years followed of which no trace remains. Geology was happening but the story has not been preserved at Chiricahua National Monument.

The next series of events to be recorded as rocks visible in the monument today were volcanic eruptions. Predating the eruptions from the Turkey Creek caldera by about forty-five million years, these eruptions created a series of rock layers, now known as the Nipper Formation, above the ancient limestones. The source for these volcanic rocks was probably somewhere in southwestern New Mexico.

Some time later, about twenty-eight to thirty million years ago, several canyons in the vicinity of what we now call Bonita Park were blocked off by faulting or volcanic deposition. Water could no longer flow to the valley below, and a deep, narrow lake filled the canyons. Sediments from the surrounding peaks and slopes accumulated in the lake to a depth of 300 feet. Eventually, volcanic deposits covered the lake-bed sediments and compacted them into conglomerates, sandstones, and siltstones. Erosion exposed these ancient lake beds, which are the red rocks visible at Bonita Park and along the road to Massai Point.

About twenty-seven million years ago, a second series of volcanic eruptions produced the Faraway Ranch Formation, which underlies the Rhyolite Canyon Formation. The location of these eruptions may have been near Portal on the southeastern side of the Chiricahua Mountains. The Faraway Ranch Formation includes nine members, mainly various types of volcanic rocks. Most of these were not produced by eruptions of the *nuée ardente* type. Instead, the source volcano disgorged viscous,

tonguelike masses of lava that crept or rolled across the ground. The most prominent member of the Faraway Ranch Formation, a rhyodacite flow, is exposed at Cochise Head and above the visitor center.

Considerable erosion of the Nipper and Faraway Ranch formations occurred before the next recorded event in Chiricahua National Monument—the eruptions from the Turkey Creek caldera about twenty-five million years ago. These occurred over a period of something less than a million years, and when they were over, they had created a rock layer nearly 2,000 feet thick.

# AFTER THE CALDERA

About fifteen million years ago, block faulting built the Chiricahua Mountains and many other mountain ranges in the Southwest. Tremendous forces within the earth began pushing some layers of rock upward and dropping adjacent layers down. Over several million years, the Chiricahua Mountains were lifted to a height much greater than their present 9,796 feet.

It's all been downhill from there, as erosion stripped away the exposed rock. Bit by bit, the mountain buried itself in its own detritus as sand, gravel, pebbles, rocks,

---

At thirteen miles in diameter, the Turkey Creek caldera is small compared to the largest one known, Sumatra's Toba caldera, which stretches sixty-two miles from wall to wall. Both are resurgent calderas, born when molten rock, or magma, rises from deep within the earth into solid rock near the surface. As the magma accumulates, it lifts the ground overhead into a dome. Upheaval splits and cracks the rocks around the edge of the dome, forming a ring-shaped fracture. Magma underneath the dome explodes from several points along the ring fracture—the *nuée ardentes* eruptions. So forceful are the eruptions that they empty the pocket of magma beneath the dome. Within hours or even minutes of the eruptions, the dome starts to collapse, creating the caldera. Continuing eruptions fill the caldera and blanket the surrounding countryside. Eventually, perhaps after a few hundred thousand years, magma again pools beneath the caldera, and its floor again rises into a dome. This is the resurgence that gives these calderas their name.

and boulders accumulated in the surrounding valleys, a process that continues today. At the same time, the caldera was bisected by the canyon we now call Turkey Creek, and as the canyon grew deeper, the distinctive features of the caldera were largely lost but for remnants of its walls here and there in adjacent canyons.

Uplifting of the Chiricahua Mountains imposed tremendous stresses on the bedrock. Under the strain, the layers of welded rhyolite tuff in the Rhyolite Canyon Formation split into huge, upright blocks. Water trickled into the cracks between the blocks and seeped into the soft zones of no welding and partial welding. As water and ice ate away at these softer zones, rock particles worked loose, then washed or fell away, creating ever larger spaces between the blocks. Over millions of years, erosion continued vertically along the fractures and horizontally along the soft zones, carving solid bedrock into rectangular pillars and eventually into spires, chess pieces, and Easter Island figures. Chiricahua National Monument is, more than anything else, a monument to erosion, to its power and the beauty it inadvertently creates.

# THE SETTING

# ISLANDS IN THE SKY

It takes less than an hour to hike the short trail to the top of Sugarloaf Mountain. Cicadas stridulate from every shrub and tree, a metallic vibrato like strummed wire. Sometimes they unnerve me by shrieking as they dart across my path. A turkey vulture coasts by, as silent as its shadow which undulates over the oaks and pines. Accustomed as I am to seeing vultures far in the sky above me, it's startling to be on the same level with one. Binoculars bring the vulture so close that I can admire the velvety blackness of its wings and notice that its body forms a keel.

As I near the apex of the conical peak, one Weidemeyer's admiral after another flies from its perch to investigate me. These beautiful black and white butterflies are probably hilltopping males. They sit alertly on the tips of oak branches, one butterfly per tree. From these lookout posts, they sally forth to investigate every passerby, either defending their tiny territories or seeking mates.

Crowning Sugarloaf Mountain is a lookout post of another sort, a one-room cabin, its four sides constructed of glass instead of logs—a fire lookout. From the top of Sugarloaf, I travel in imagination across the blue peaks that punctuate the horizon. Going west, I skim across the Sonoran Desert, looking down on tall, many-armed saguaro cacti and resinous-leaved creosote bush. Traveling east, I glide for many miles above the Chihuahuan Desert, where the creosote bush again holds sway for vast distances. Heading north, I must let my imagination soar so that I can rise over the Rocky Mountains, over the snow-splashed peaks and flower-filled meadows, and traveling south, I find myself looking down on the Sierra Madre Occidental, the Mexican extension of the Rocky Mountains, where parrots flock among the pines.

Returning to earth, I take in the landscape that surrounds me, a vast circular platter with an overturned blue bowl for a lid. Looking eastwards, I see the San Simon Valley, straw-colored in the gauzy light of a midsummer morning. To the west the Sulphur Springs Valley spreads out in the sun like melted butter. To the north, the prominent feature known as Cochise Head stares forever at the sky. Its hawk-nosed, stern-browed profile evidently reminded its namer of the Apache Indian warrior Cochise. Also to the north and a bit farther west are the Dos Cabezas Mountains, indigo blue near the top where woodland cloaks the slopes. Looking south, I see the dark, forested spine of the Chiricahua Mountains, which continues nearly to the Mexican border, and I remember that the 12,000 acres circumscribed by Chiricahua National Monument are only a portion of this mountain range. Rising from an elevation of 5,000 feet at the base to 9,796 feet on Chiricahua Peak, the Chiricahua Mountains take in some 325,000 acres and dominate the skyline for miles around. Separated from neighboring mountain ranges by arid expanses of desert and grassland, they stand above the surrounding plain much as an oceanic island rises from the sea. For this reason, the Chiricahua Mountains and other ranges in the Southwest are often called sky islands.

A sky island is first of all a climatic island. As you ascend the Chiricahua Mountains, you climb through several different climates—from hot summers and cool winters at the bottom to mild summers and frigid winters at the top. When a summer day at the bottom brings temperatures of 100 degrees, the temperature will be a pleasant eighty degrees higher up. When winter temperatures on the mountaintop drop to zero, the temperature at the base of the range might hover around the freezing point. Rainfall increases as you progress up a mountain, as do the number of cloudy and foggy days. In the Chiricahua Mountains, precipitation at the base is about fifteen inches annually, while at the top of the range, more than twice that falls.

A sky island is a biotic island, too. We can't see the climatic zones that ring this sky island, but we can see the belts of vegetation that correspond to each zone. In the Chiricahua Mountains, the lowest belt, grassland, surrounds the range. It grades upwards into a woodland of oaks, pines, and junipers, which gives way to a forest of pines, which in turn grades into a forest of firs, Douglas-firs, and spruces. Many miles of desert or grassland separate the belts of woodland and forest in the Chiricahua Mountains from similar belts on nearby ranges. The animals within each belt are also isolated from their fellows on other sky islands. Birds can fly from one mountain range to the next, but most insects and reptiles are incapable of such sustained travel. Mammals, too, except for a few of the largest ones, do not cross the sea of desert or grassland that separates their particular sky island from the others.

# AUTUMN COMES IN APRIL

The song of a black-headed grosbeak greets me as I step from the sunlit parking lot at the visitor center into the shadowy forest in the bottom of Rhyolite Canyon. I look for the grosbeak but can't find him; his song seems to come from everywhere at once. There's no mistaking the clearly articulated, alternately rising and falling notes; it's a birdlike version of French. At last I spy him, a brilliant orange and black bird with a chunky bill, on a low branch in an Emory oak. As he flies away, I catch a glimpse of his white wing bars.

It's June, and fire danger is high. A sign at the trailhead warns against smoking on the trail. As I scuffle through the thick carpet of leaves on the ground, I can see why. Oak leaves crackle underfoot, stems snap, pine needles rustle. There are more leaves on the ground than above it. The accumulation of litter is dry enough to fuel a summer-long bonfire.

Last month this canyon-bottom forest of oaks and pines did look as though wildfire had swept through. Some of the oaks, their leaves having turned brown, copper, or bronze, appeared scorched. Others, having lost all their leaves, looked more like pencil sketches of trees than the real thing.

Every year in April and May, these oaks discard old leaves for new. As the old leaves fall, soft, fuzzy shoots appear at the branch tips. The inconspicuous flower tassels that dangle from the new branchlets give every oak a golden nimbus. Tiny, furled leaves soon appear, and, in a matter of six weeks or so, the transformation from an autumnal landscape to a vernal one is complete.

Here in Chiricahua National Monument, the seasons don't match the calendar divisions of spring, summer, fall, and winter. Instead, there are two rainy seasons, one warm, one cold, separated by two dry seasons, one hot, one warm.

The seasonal rise and fall of temperatures, the moistening and drying of the soil, the changing lengths of days and nights, the steady rains of winter, the drenching thunderstorms of summer, the hot high peaks and the short sharp lows on the temperature chart: all these determine how the plants and animals at the monument behave throughout the year and even, to some extent, determine what plants and animals occur in the monument.

The climate at Chiricahua National Monument is generally mild. In the summer, temperatures rarely exceed 100 degrees, although a sizzling 109 degrees was recorded in July 1909. June is typically the hottest month with an average temperature of seventy-six degrees Fahrenheit. Winter temperatures regularly drop to thirty-two degrees and below, especially in January, the coldest month. The

Almost anywhere you go in Chiricahua National Monument, your eyes are bound to fall upon an oak. Seven species of oaks grow within the monument's boundaries, and all but one, the Gambel oak, are common. The inconspicuous oak blossoms are fertilized as wind blows pollen from male to female catkins. Pollination by wind works best when individuals are abundant and reasonably close together, as is true of oaks in woodland and forest. Also, wind pollination is most efficient when there are few leaves to intercept the airborne pollen. In southeastern Arizona, oaks (with the exception of Gambel oak) drop their leaves in the spring, just before the flowers release their pollen. Gambel oak, a fall-deciduous tree, also blooms before it puts out new leaves.

lowest temperature on record, minus ten degrees Fahrenheit, occurred in January 1913, but it is rare for temperatures to drop below zero degrees.

Annual precipitation averages eighteen inches but varies greatly from year to year. In the driest year on record, 1970, only 9.8 inches of rain fell; in the wettest year, 1983, precipitation was nearly thirty-two inches. Trace amounts of snow have been recorded in every month. December and January are the snowiest months. At lower elevations, snow melts rapidly. Higher up, it may linger for a week or two on shaded slopes.

Even more important than the averages of temperature and totals of precipitation is their distribution throughout the year. Twenty-seven percent of the precipitation falls in the cooler months, from December through March. These winter storms blow in from the Pacific Ocean and generally cover a broad area. Because most plants are dormant or nearly so in the winter, their consumption of water is minimal, and because temperatures are low, little moisture evaporates from the upper layers of soil. Winter rains and snows, therefore, soak into the ground.

This stored moisture is available to plants once temperatures rise in April. There is a flush of growth as trees and shrubs put forth flowers and new leaves. The abundant soil moisture means that plants can keep their leaf pores open all day long. Although they lose water this way, they compensate by being able to photosynthesize the sugars needed for producing new leaves and flowers.

By June, this growth spurt ceases as the soil dries out. A mere seven percent of the yearly rain comes in the warm months of April, May, and June. In some years, no rain at all is recorded in these months. Temperatures climb high enough that plants are in danger of losing too much water to the air, and they must make corresponding adjustments in the length of time they can keep their pores open for photosynthesis.

Soil moisture is replenished once again when the

summer rains come. Fifty-five percent of the yearly precipitation falls in July, August, and September, when temperatures are high. Summer rains usually start in early July as a tongue of moist air spreads north from the Gulf of Mexico, developing into thunderstorms over the high mountain ranges. These scattered storms are crashing, drenching affairs in which an inch of rain may fall in an hour. The normally dry streambeds rumble as water cascades from cliffs and canyon slopes into the drainage channels; then, in several hours or days, most of the water will have disappeared, leaving only occasional pools to hint at the recent torrents. In response to summer rains, the grasses sprout new leaves and, in a matter of weeks, tawny hillsides and pastures turn green. Wildflowers, too, take advantage of this warm, wet season; August and September are the best months for wildflowers at Chiricahua National Monument. Many shrubs put on a second set of flowers in response to summer rains.

October and November, like April, May, and June, are typically on the dry side; only ten percent of the annual precipitation falls in these months. The drying trend of autumn causes soil moisture to drop once again. In combination with the cooling temperatures, this signals plants to shut down for the winter until rising temperatures in spring bring them to life.

# CLIMATES WITHIN CLIMATES

Standing in the bottom of Rhyolite Canyon, I am struck by the difference between the two sides of the canyon. On the wall facing south, a woodland of small trees dots the slope and spills among loose boulders nearly to the canyon bottom. On the opposite side of the canyon, a forest of tall trees flourishes.

**BLACK-CHINNED HUMMINGBIRD**

These opposing slopes exist under the same regional climate but their day-to-day climate differs appreciably. Such variations of a regional climate are called microclimates. The south-facing slope of Rhyolite Canyon has an arid microclimate compared with the north-facing slope. Because the southern slope bakes under a high level of solar radiation while the northern slope is shaded during much of the day, soil and air temperatures are higher on southern than on northern slopes. Also, evaporation from the soil and water loss by plants are greater on the hotter slope.

I hear the metallic trill of a broad-tailed hummingbird as he flashes by. I wonder what he is finding to eat during these dry June days. Like all hummingbirds, the broad-tailed lives largely on flower nectar, and I have seen few flowers in bloom today. Walking a bit further up Rhyolite Canyon, I arrive at a rock outcrop and an answer at the same time. A clump of cactus—the claret-cup hedgehog—blooms lustily on the rocks. Its vermillion flowers gape to reveal the dense brush of yellow stamens and green stigmas inside. A hummingbird darts up to the flowers and probes them quickly and efficiently, her wings beating so rapidly that they blur.

Seeing the hedgehog reminds me that not all plants prefer moist, cool microclimates. Some, like claret-cup hedgehog, require warmer and drier conditions than even a south-facing slope affords. Cacti are relatively sensitive to freezing temperatures, and although this cactus is less sensitive than most, it still requires amelioration of the coldest winter temperatures. On sunny days, cliffs and boulders absorb the heat of the sun, then radiate warmth at night. This extra bit of heat is just enough to prevent frost damage to the tender cactus tissues on the coldest nights. Frost-sensitive plants like claret-cup hedgehog seldom grow at the bottoms of canyons, where cold air accumulates at night; rather, they thrive on canyon slopes and walls, where the minimum temperature may be five or ten degrees higher than on the canyon floor.

North-facing slopes have one climate, south-facing slopes another. Cliff faces, deeply shaded canyon bottoms, and exposed ridges present even more sets of climatic conditions. What plants and animals perceive, then, is not the single, uniform climate measured by the meteorologist but a mosaic of microclimates.

# THE PLANTS AND ANIMALS

# A WALK IN THE WOODLAND: BIOTIC COMMUNITIES OF CHIRICAHUA NATIONAL MONUMENT

It's early morning in mid-July. The day, already warm, promises to be hot later on. Today I am hiking down the Echo Canyon Loop trail to Echo Park and back along the Hailstone Trail. As I know from previous trips, this is one of the most varied hikes in the monument, in part because it traverses four of the monument's six biotic communities: chaparral, mixed conifer forest, pine-oak woodland, and oak woodland.

A biotic community is simply a group of plant and animal species that regularly occur together. I can hardly imagine a woodland of oaks without its accompanying gray-breasted jays, for example, nor a forest of ponderosa pines without some Steller's jays. The mosaic of biotic communities in the monument corresponds to the mosaic of microclimates. With every twist and turn in the landscape, the biotic community changes as plants respond to windy exposures, sheltered coves, shaded nooks, sunny slopes, bare rock, damp humus, and a hundred other situations. In most places it is difficult or even impossible to draw sharp boundaries between adjacent biotic communities. Each community grades imperceptibly into the next, and many species occur in several communities.

## Chaparral

From the parking lot, the Echo Canyon Loop trail conducts me though waist-high thickets of manzanita and Toumey oak. If I could float above the shrubbery, I would see a pattern of circular splotches, like full skirts dropped to the ground. Progress through these thickets would be impossible without a trail, for the branches are locked together as firmly as the steel strands of a chain-link fence. Mexican pinyon, Arizona cypress, alligator juniper, and Emory oak emerge above the shrubbery. This community is more like chaparral than woodland in the prevalence of such thicket-forming shrubs as manzanita and Toumey oak and more like woodland than true chaparral in the abundance of dwarfed trees. (More typical chaparral occurs along the Natural Bridge trail.)

Chaparral is one of the most drought-tolerant biotic communities in the monument. It grows on exposed ridges where solar radiation is high and wind is nearly constant. The combination of heat and wind results in quick evaporation of soil moisture and high rates of water loss from plants. Many chaparral plants, particularly the manzanitas and oaks, possess tough, leathery leaves that resist water loss.

A crashing in the undergrowth startles me at first: it sounds like a bear breaking through the manzanitas. When I hear a drawn-out, plaintive call, I realize that it's only a rufous-sided towhee foraging for insects and seeds by kicking aside leaves and pine needles. Since these birds spend so much time in the undergrowth, they are more often heard than seen. Unlike their complaining call, their song—two or three staccato notes followed by a prolonged trill—is loud, clear, and optimistic.

Someone nearby is scolding me with sharp, shrill yips: on a fallen log, a cliff chipmunk twitches its tail with every squeak. (According to my field guide, they bark up to 160 times a minute.) Cliff chipmunks eat a variety of seeds and berries, particularly manzanita berries. They'll climb high into trees to harvest walnuts, juniper berries, and acorns. Although they don't hibernate in the winter, they do become inactive when snow covers the ground. Stored food tides them over these periods when they can't forage regularly.

## Airshafts and Litter Shadows

Continuing along the trail, I eventually find myself in a city of rocks. Columns carved from buff-colored rhyolite tower overhead like skyscrapers. Walking down the shadowy corridors, I hear the liquid laugh of a canyon wren, eight or ten clear, sweet notes descending the scale and ending in a raucous raspberry. So faithfully is the canyon wren associated with cliffs, its song almost seems to be the voice of the rocks themselves. Soon I see a pair of the wrens bobbing on a narrow ledge above me. Their white bibs are conspicuous as they step into a shaft of sunlight, as are their long bills and flattened heads. The Papago and Pima Indians called this bird the flat-headed wren; they say that its head got stepped on at a wine feast. The canyon wren's long bill and flattened head are useful for searching out insects in rock crevices.

As I put down my binoculars, a violet-green swallow dives by me so rapidly I nearly lose my balance. Glancing into the airshafts between the pillars, I see a mixed flock of violet-green swallows and white-throated swifts. The swifts chitter excitedly: their high-pitched voices sound like a distant schoolyard full of children. Gliding, turning, twisting, swooping, and, miraculously, never colliding, swifts and swallows continually forage for air-borne insects. The air is their natural medium, especially for the swifts, which have such weakly developed legs they can hardly walk. They even mate on the wing. Violet-green swallows, summer residents at Chiricahua National Monument, nest in tree cavities or in cracks in cliffs. The white-throated swifts are year-round residents here. They nest far inside crevices in cliffs.

Ordinarily, chaparral is a blanket of vegetation, but among these pillars, where soil is thin or nonexistent, it is more like a cloak of loosely joined patches. One typical patch here includes a Toumey oak, a silver-leaf oak, two Parry agaves, a clump of beargrass, and three seedlings of Mexican pinyon. Another contains a spreading

Manzanita, Spanish for "little apple," is named for the small, mealy berries which ripen in the summer. Like many fleshy fruits, the little apples of manzanita depend on animals for dispersal. When bears or chipmunks or birds eat the berries, the seeds pass through their digestive tracts unharmed and emerge ready to germinate.

Manzanita also propagates without seeds. Branches pressed against the ground take root, forming new plants. This cluster of plants is a clone, each genetically identical to the others. Eventually the center of the clone dies, leaving a ring of younger plants. Theoretically, a clone could live forever as successive generations put forth new plants of their own. In practice, most clones probably die in wildfires before they attain the century mark.

Fire is a friend as well as a foe to manzanita. After the heat of a blaze cracks the thick seed coat, water can penetrate into the seed and initiate germination. Manzanita germinates abundantly after a fire, as do many other chaparral plants. This is an important adaptation in a community where wildfires are frequent and intense.

point-leaf manzanita, a Mexican pinyon, and a young Toumey oak.

I scrape the ground with the toe of my boot, scuffing up sand and gravel. The soil is hardly developed at all; it consists mostly of rock fragments. Because of the lack of humus—rotted organic matter—precipitation isn't held as soil moisture; instead, it simply flows downslope. Also, solar radiation is high on these exposed slopes, so the ground is quite warm during the summer months. The lack of moisture and the high temperatures impede seedling establishment. The only place where seedlings find the moisture and shade they need is in the protection of full-grown plants, where fallen leaves form a "litter shadow." A seedling is much more likely to become established within a chaparral patch, therefore, than on open ground.

## Mixed Conifer Forest
It is windy up here among the rock pillars. Gusts ruffle the pages of my notebook and throb against my ears. I glance up, half-expecting to see the rock towers swaying, as the tallest skyscrapers are said to do in gales, but these sky towers are motionless. I'm glad when the trail drops down from the windy city into a side canyon. Here, just a hundred feet below the rim of the canyon, the air is still.

That's not all that has changed. The scrubby chaparral of the ridges has given way to a shaded forest. It changed so gradually that I didn't notice it until I felt cool shade on my face instead of warm sun. In the chaparral on the ridge above, the tallest trees hardly exceeded me in height. Here the pinyons and oaks are twenty feet tall, and farther below me, in the canyon bottom, Arizona cypresses and ponderosa pines have attained majestic heights of sixty feet or more. Going from the ridge into this steep, narrow side canyon, I have descended a graduated scale where the increments are marked in moisture and temperature. Chaparral occurs towards the dry, warm end of the scale; mixed conifer forest towards the moist, cool end.

Arriving on the canyon floor, I take off my pack and plop onto a boulder for a sip of water from my canteen. As I sit quietly, the forest birds resume their regular tasks. Movement on the trunk of a nearby oak catches my eye. Cautiously I turn my head to see a streaky brown, spindle-shaped bird spiraling up the trunk with abrupt hops: a brown creeper, searching for insects on the bark.

Hot and sweaty as I was on the ridge above, I am now almost chilly as a gentle breeze presses my damp shirt against my back. Looking around, I admire the tall forest trees in this mixed conifer forest: Arizona cypress, with finely striated bark; red-branched madrone, one of Arizona's most beautiful forest trees; ponderosa pine with its plated bark; and an occasional Douglas-fir loaded with sticky, green cones. All but the madrone are conifers. The deep shade makes this canyon bottom appreciably cooler year-round than the slopes and ridges above. Here winter snows remain on the ground for several weeks at a time, soaking into the soil and providing plenty of moisture to tide these forest trees over the hot, dry days of May and June.

## Pine-Oak Woodland
From Echo Park the trail continues along the bottom of Echo Canyon through a woodland of net-leaf oak, silver-leaf oak, Arizona oak, Apache pine, Chihuahua pine, Mexican pinyon, alligator juniper, and Arizona cypress. This pine-oak woodland grades into mixed conifer forest toward the moist end of the scale and into oak woodland at the dry end. In the monument, pine-oak woodland thrives in canyon bottoms and on north-facing slopes. Solar radiation is less intense in these locations than on ridges or south-facing slopes, so soil and plants lose less water. Also, the leaf and needle litter that accumulates in thick pads on the forest floor decays into humus, which

retains soil moisture much better than the mineral soil of the ridges.

No stream fills the rocky channel in Echo Canyon. After the summer rains start, water will tumble over and around these rocks, but for now there are only small pools where the dark water moves so slowly it scarcely stirs the streamers of algae on the bottom. An orange dragonfly patrols one short stretch of water, returning always to its perch on a dead twig that overhangs the streambed. Water striders skate on the suface of a pool, and below them, backswimmers sink and rise like tiny yo-yos.

The trail crosses the streambed by a gravelly pool. As my shadow falls onto the water, a dozen tadpoles dart away. They are, I believe, canyon tree frogs, a common amphibian of streambed pools in the mountains throughout the Southwest. In spring and summer male tree frogs utter bleating, sheeplike calls meant to attract females. When frogs mate, the males grab the females and sit on top of them. Mating is complicated by the male frog's propensity to grab any moving object; as often as not, this proves to be another male rather than a female, resulting in brief but intense struggles.

Turning a bend in the trail, I interrupt three or four courting couples—all painted redstarts. The females fly from branch to branch as the males pursue them. Whenever a female perches on a low branch, a male lands beside her, spreads his wings, and fans his tail. This posture displays to good advantage the white bars on his black wings and the white stripes along the sides of his black tail. Every so often I glimpse a male's blood-red breast, a startling contrast to his somber black and white color scheme. It's like seeing red socks on an otherwise properly attired mortician.

## Oak Woodland

Before too long the Echo Canyon Loop Trail joins the Hailstone Trail. In Echo Canyon, the trail clung to the shaded, north-facing slopes. Here on the Hailstone Trail it strikes across the warm, sunny, south-facing slope of Rhyolite Canyon. Toumey oak, Emory oak, Mexican pinyon, and alligator juniper grow dwarfed on this drier slope; most are no more than fifteen feet tall. Mixed with the trees are a variety of shrubs and succulents. In

---

The idea of a rock garden takes on a whole new meaning at Chiricahua National Monument, where some plants literally grow out of bare rock. Cascading branches of apacheria, yellow pincushions of Cochise rock daisy, neat tufts of pine-leaf penstemon sporting red flowers like tiny banners, starry clumps of sedum, cheery bunches of golden aster, spiky mounds of claret-cup hedgehog: these and other plants thrive best on the vertical surfaces of cliffs and boulder piles.

First lichens, then mosses, pave the way for these rock-dwelling wildflowers. Lichens dissolve the rock, eventually providing enough soil that mosses find a foothold. More soil accumulates among the rootlets of the moss clumps, and when a seed of apacheria or Cochise rock daisy or another rock plant lands on the moss, it finds a tiny pocket of moist soil where it can germinate and grow. Roots of these rock plants insinuate themselves into slight cracks in the boulders where they extract mineral nutrients and water.

Some of these rock plants are rare. Apacheria is known only from the monument and two or three other locations. Although it was collected in the monument in the late 1930s, it wasn't recognized as a new species for nearly forty years. So far, Cochise rock daisy has not been found anywhere but Chiricahua National Monument.

ACORN WOODPECKER

hawking perches, and roosts. These requirements reflect the seasonal food habits of the acorn woodpecker. During fall and winter, they feed extensively on acorns and also store many acorns in specially prepared holes in trunks and branches. (These are the marble-sized holes in the uppermost branches of many snags.) The stored acorns usually provide enough food to last into the spring, when insects become a major food item. Spring is the nesting period, and like most baby birds, acorn woodpecker nestlings thrive best on a diet of insects. Instead of boring for insects in trunks as do other woodpeckers, acorn woodpeckers hawk insects out of the air. Often a parent will accumulate captured insects in storage holes, then carry them in a batch to the nestlings. The third major food source for acorn woodpeckers, sap, is most important in the early summer. By the end of the summer, green acorns are available again, and the woodpeckers split them and eat the meat from the inside.

After a minute or two, the woodpeckers glide upslope to a cluster of Douglas-firs at the base of a cliff. Even on an arid south-facing slope like this one, moist spots in the shade of a cliff create a microclimate within a microclimate. Snow remains longer here, providing extra soil moisture in the spring for the moisture-loving Douglas-fir. Also, air and soil temperatures are somewhat lower because of the shade, resulting in lower rates of water loss from soil and plants.

I stop to adjust my bootlace. Bending over, I realize that I am eye to eye with a Yarrow's spiny lizard. When I lean forward to get a closer look, it darts under its rock. A moment later it emerges and inches towards me. Its back is irridescently colored in dark hues: bronze, black, and red. As one biologist wrote, it looks as though it is wearing a lace body stocking. Erect, pointed scales give it a rough, spiny appearance.

Like many other lizards in southwestern woodlands, the Yarrow's spiny lizard feeds primarily on insects,

this oak woodland trees are smaller and farther apart than in pine-oak woodland, and taller and closer together than in chaparral.

An acorn woodpecker glides in for a landing at the top of a nearby snag. The white patches on wings and rump make it easy to recognize. Through my binoculars I see its clownlike white and black face and red pate. "Jacob, Jacob," it shouts, a harsh call that sounds like a squeaking bedspring. In a moment, a second woodpecker joins it.

Acorn woodpeckers are communal breeders. The flocks of two to ten birds include both sexes and varying ages. All members of the flock assist with defending the territory, constructing nest holes, and feeding nestlings.

A good territory for a flock of acorn woodpeckers covers a minimum of five acres and includes oaks for acorn harvesting, one or more trees suitable for acorn storage, and additional trees containing nest holes, sap, especially ants, flies, beetles, grasshoppers, and crickets. These lizards are visibly active during the warm months. In the winter they forage only on warm days and are inactive much of the time.

The lizard does push-ups at me to mark its territory. Yarrow's spiny lizards maintain feeding territories which they defend against adult lizards of the same sex and all juveniles. Defense is fairly mild by human standards: besides doing push-ups, they bob their heads, inflate their throats, step sideways, lash their tails, and, in extreme circumstances, bite.

Most lizards hatch from eggs laid in underground nests. The warmth of the soil fosters development of the embryo inside the egg. Yarrow's spiny lizard is unusual in bearing its young alive. Although males inseminate females in the fall, the fertilized eggs don't develop into embryos until the following spring. This schedule permits the young to be born in June when food is plentiful. Also, it spares females the stress of supporting developing embryos during the winter, when insects are scarce and adult food intake is limited. Certain other lizards found in the monument also bear their young alive, among them the bunch grass lizard and the short-horned lizard.

The trail eventually turns up a side canyon shaded by oaks and cypresses, and I am in pine-oak woodland again. A California sister, a butterfly with an orange and white exclamation point on each brown wing, floats down the canyon, then settles on an oak leaf. Most oaks contain bitter chemicals, called tannins, which make the leaves inedible. A few insects, however, have evolved a tolerance to tannins, among them the California sister, whose caterpillars feed on oak leaves.

Bright colors—red and yellow—on the brown leaf litter attract my attention, then resolve themselves into a slender snake that slides as silently as a thought over the leaves and behind a log. Quickly, before it disappears, I check the pattern of the red, yellow, and black bands, and determine that it is a Sonoran mountain kingsnake. (On the venomous Arizona coral snake, the red bands are bordered by yellow; on the nonvenomous kingsnake, red bands are bordered by black.)

Most snakes around here blend in with their surroundings, but the brilliantly-colored Sonoran mountain kingsnake stands out. Some biologists have suggested that the innocuous kingsnake's bright color pattern evolved to mimic that of the poisonous coral snake. Animals with

One of the most remarkable lizards in Chiricahua National Monument is the Chihuahua whiptail, a sleek lizard striped with yellow and brown. These whiptails live in oak woodland, often along stream bottoms. Speedy runners, they dart readily for cover when disturbed. They feed primarily on insects, spiders, and scorpions, sometimes locating their prey underground by smell. The Chihuahua whiptail is one of thirteen species of whiptail lizards that are entirely female. They reproduce not by intercourse but by parthenogenesis: young develop from unfertilized eggs and are clones of the parent.

SONORAN MOUNTAIN KINGSNAKE

# BONITA CANYON: MORE BIOTIC COMMUNITIES

### Meadow

After supper, I stroll from the campground to Silver Spur Meadow, where, swatting an occasional mosquito, I wade through knee-high grasses. Their golden seed heads shimmer in the slanting shafts of late afternoon sunlight and bobble in the wind. This end of the meadow is dry; bare, cracked soil shows between the clumps of grass. Once summer rains moisten the earth, wildflowers—goldenrod, mullein, horsetail milkweed, and fleabane—will spring up among the grasses. Along the edge of the meadow, long, low mounds of earth that look like vacuum cleaner hoses remind me that the pocket gopher is the common resident mammal of Silver Spur Meadow.

As I walk toward the western end of the meadow, I step gingerly to avoid sinking ankle-deep into the runnels of water. Stems of scouring rush clink as I walk through them. The silica contained in the cells not only makes them clink but also makes them rough enough to use as scouring pads. In this part of the meadow grasses give way to sedges, spike-rushes, and true rushes. Wet meadows can be found in the monument only at Silver Spur Meadow and at one or two other permanent springs. Only where water is available all year can semi-aquatic plants and animals such as the spike-rushes and garter snakes survive.

### Riparian Forest

Silver Spur Meadow spills over an embankment into Bonita Creek. It's just a few steps from one to the other. Surface water is sporadic at Chiricahua National Monument. Just as soil on slopes and flats undergoes seasonal fluctuations in moisture, so does that of streambeds. None of the canyons in the monument support perma-

color vision learn that red-and-black-patterned organisms are often venomous. Alerted by its warning colors, predators tend to leave coral snakes alone. This permits the snake to conserve its venom for hunting, instead of expending it on defense. By imitating the colors of the Arizona coral snake, the Sonoran mountain kingsnake gains some protection from potential predators that mistakenly (but prudently) believe it to be dangerous.

Not all biologists would agree that the coral snake bears warning coloration and that the kingsnake mimics it. One biologist has suggested that at night, when these snakes are most active, the alternating light and dark bands produce a blur of gray and black that blends with leaf litter on the ground. Thus the striking color pattern actually acts as camouflage.

nent streams, although there are several year-round springs, like the one in Silver Spur Meadow. Only in extraordinarily wet years does the creek in Bonita Canyon flow in all twelve months. In most years, the seasons of flow correspond roughly to the rainy seasons: July to October and February to April. Now, in early summer, the creek is not running, but shallow pools in the streambed teem with life.

These springs and streambed pools are good places to observe such aquatic insects as dragonflies, damselflies, water striders, and backswimmers, and aquatic animals like garter snakes, canyon tree frogs, and southwestern leopard frogs. Mosquitoes harrass me as I sit on a rock to watch the whirligig beetles frenetically spinning. Blue damselflies, joined in pairs, are plentiful. The male is always the front member of every pair. He holds the female by clasping her neck with the tip of his tail. Thus connected, they skim over the water, pausing every so often on twigs or leaves for the female to lay her eggs.

At my feet, water-loving sedges, rushes, and horsetails edge the streambed pools. Overhead a canopy of sycamore leaves shades me from the sun. Sycamore is just one of the large trees that grows along the streambed in lower Bonita Canyon. Other trees in this riparian forest community include velvet ash, walnut, and an occasional cottonwood, all deciduous trees. Arizona cypress, another common streamside tree here, is evergreen. These water-loving trees require more moisture than is found even on constantly shaded slopes. Growing along the banks of on-again-off-again creeks, they use both intermittent stream flow and water stored underground between the gravels and cobbles of the stream channel.

I had half-hoped to hear or see elegant trogons, which nest in holes in sycamores, but I have no luck. These beautiful birds occur in the monument only sporadically. In Cave Creek, on the eastern side of the Chiricahua Mountains, they can be found every year between May and September.

A deeply incised pawprint in the mud catches my eye. It looks a bit like the prints my cat makes when she walks with muddy feet across the hood of my car, except that this one is nearly twice as large and the marks of claws are clearly visible. After leafing through my field guide, I decide that it is most likely the track of a coatimundi, which, like its relative the racoon, is often found near water.

A thoroughly omnivorous animal, the coatimundi will eat anything that doesn't eat it first: insects, spiders, worms, lizards, snakes, rodents, carrion, garbage, juniper berries, manzanita berries, prickly pears, acorns, apples, peaches, and garden vegetables are some of the items in a typical coati diet. They forage like skunks— noses to the ground, tails in the air, shuffling and scuffling to scare up dinner from the leaf litter. Unlike skunks, which are solitary, coatis forage in bands of four to forty. These bands comprise several females and their immature offspring. Mature males are solitary wanderers, coming together with others of their kind only to mate.

In Arizona, coatimundis have been spotted in a range of habitats, from desert to mountaintop, but they are most often seen among oaks and pines. Unlike many mammals, coatis are nomadic. They tend to work one canyon complex, then move on when they have exhausted the local food supplies.

### Grassland

If I followed the creekbed downstream to the mouth of Bonita Canyon where the canyon walls fall away, I would see a sweeping view of blue sky and tawny grassland to the west. At Chiricahua National Monument, grassland occurs on gentle slopes and plains along the western boundary. The grasses—blue grama, side-oats grama, black grama, wolf-tail, panic grass, love grass, and many others—are straw-colored much of the year, but once summer rains arrive, they green up with new leaves and shoots in a matter of weeks. In spring and summer, wild-flowers abound in the grassland: Indian paintbrush, summer poppy, plains zinnia, moss rose, California poppy, locoweed, sacred datura, mariposa lily, and dakota verbena. Many small cacti nestle among the rocks. Blue-green rosettes of Palmer agave lift candelabras of seed pods towards the sun.

If I stayed out here until dark, I might see a desert pocket mouse, a Merriam's kangaroo rat, or a northern grasshopper mouse, three of the many rodents that live in the grassland. Grasshopper mice eat insects and can even kill small mammals up to their own size. Pocket mice and kangaroo rats are seed-eaters; while foraging at night, they pack their cheek pockets full of seed to take back to their burrows. Kangaroo rats bounce on their hind legs from place to place, whereas pocket mice, like any ordinary mouse, scamper on all four feet. Like most rodents, these have nervous dispositions, and they quickly take cover when alarmed. Their many enemies include owls, bobcats, snakes, mountain lions, foxes, coyotes, skunks, and badgers.

Of all the biotic communities in the monument, grassland has probably been most altered by human activity. Early on, settlers turned cattle loose to graze on grassy slopes and plains. As livestock multiplied, they exceeded the capacity of the land to support them, and in many places, overgrazing, shrub invasion, and erosion were the result. Signs of overgrazing include pastures thick with prickly poppy, Lambert locoweed, and long-leaf groundsel, none of which cattle will eat. Throughout southeastern Arizona, brushy areas where mesquite now dominates were once productive grasslands. Cattle no longer graze within the boundaries of the monument, and, with time, the overgrazed areas may recover.

# CRACKER HOARDERS AND BUTTERFLY CATCHERS: ANIMAL AND PLANT NICHES AT CHIRICAHUA NATIONAL MONUMENT

As I move about my campsite preparing breakfast—taking eggs from the ice chest, making coffee, laying bacon strips in the frying pan—a gray-breasted jay bounces along the ground behind me or glides from branch to branch in front of me. Having already learned that I am a soft touch, the bird persists until I finally toss it a piece of cracker, although I know I shouldn't. The jay approaches, picks up the cracker in its bill, and backs off. Standing with both feet on the cracker, it takes a bite from the edge, then stabs the remainder into the ground. A bit of bark placed carefully on top serves as a lid. Later in the day, I expect, the jay will unerringly relocate the cracker.

Sipping my coffee, I watch an orange butterfly—a sulphur—dally over a patch of purple verbena. Overhead, an ash-throated flycatcher perches at the top of an Emory oak. With clocklike regularity, it loops out in aerial pursuit of flying insects. Its bill clicks whenever it makes a catch. As I watch the bird through my binoculars, it sweeps toward me, and, almost before I know it, the flycatcher has captured the unwary sulphur and returned to its perch, where it gulps the butterfly, wings and all.

Burying crackers and catching butterflies are not behavioral quirks but survival tactics. Caching food is part of a gray-breasted jay's niche, just as snatching air-borne insects is part of the flycatcher's. Basically, a niche is everything that an animal does: the habitat where it lives, the food it eats, the way it forages, the seasons when it is active, the enemies it must escape, even the way it secures a mate.

In general, a species occupies a niche peculiar to itself. All rock squirrels in the monument, for example, hold the same niche, which includes a nesting site under rocks and boulders; access to pine needles, agave fiber, or grapevine bark for nesting material; and a supply of food, particularly berries, nuts, seeds, and acorns. We find rock squirrels throughout the monument wherever these requirements are met. Theoretically, no two coexisting species can occupy precisely identical niches. If they did, they would compete for the same supply of food, shelter, nesting sites, and resulting in one species outcompeting the other and gaining control of the resources.

The seasonal availability of nesting sites provides one way for birds to create unique niches. In oak woodland, most birds begin nesting in April and May as the oaks are losing their leaves. Leafless canopies make poor nesting sites because they provide protection neither from the elements nor from predators. Many birds, such as the ash-throated flycatcher, bridled titmouse, and Bewick's wren, avoid this problem by nesting in cavities. Others, including the lark sparrow and the rufous-crowned sparrow, nest on the ground. Canopy-nesting birds must either nest in evergreen trees or time their nesting to avoid the leafless period.

Another way birds partition the environment is by using different foods. Obviously some birds eat insects, others eat seeds, still others depend on flower nectar. But even more subtle distinctions exist. Among the insect eaters, some glean insects from leaves—the common bushtit, for one. Others forage on tree trunks, seeking insects on the bark, as does the bridled titmouse. Some hawk insects out of the air, as do the many kingbirds.

---

Potential competitors need not be related at all. At the monument, harvester ants, pocket mice, and sparrows all eat seeds and all live in grassland. In most years, their different food-gathering habits prevent them from competing. Because ants cannot get a firm grip on slick surfaces, they do not harvest smooth seeds. They do best with seeds that have rough coats or stiff hairs or knobby projections. Sparrows, on the other hand, prefer smooth seeds. If a seed is encased in a rough coat, the sparrow must husk the seed before eating it, whereas smooth seeds can be eaten without pretreatment. Rodents, too, tend to consume more smooth seeds than rough. Seed type, then, is one basis for niche differentiation among these grassland animals.

Their niches seem even more clearly defined when we take seasonal foraging patterns into account. Harvester ants in the grassland are most active from May through September. By mid-November, they cease foraging altogether for several months. Migrating sparrows start to arrive in the grassland in September, just before the ants become inactive, and leave for their breeding grounds in April, as the ants resume activity once again.

Clearly, harvester ants and grasshopper sparrows don't compete for food in the grassland. The biggest potential conflict would be between sparrows and rodents, since both prefer smooth seeds, and this may be a problem in years of poor rainfall when seed production is low.

---

Hummingbirds that migrate through Chiricahua National Monument in the late summer find a banquet of flowers: pine-leaved penstemon, cardinal flower, Indian pink, scarlet creeper, Rothrock thistle, Lemmon sage, betony, hummingbird-trumpet, red columbine, bouvardia, Indian paint-brush, and red penstemon.

Because these dozen wildflowers from nine different plant families evolved to attract hummingbirds as pollinators, they share certain features. All have narrow tubes that are about as long as the bills of their hummingbird pollinators. (Even the thistle contains hundreds of small flowers, each with a long, narrow tube.) Because the mouth of each flower is open, not shut tight like a snapdragon or a sweet pea, the tubes are readily accessible to a hummingbird's probing bill. Inside each flower, the stamens are arranged to dust pollen on a hummer's head, face, or chin, and the stigmas are placed to collect it when the bird visits another flower of the same type. All these flowers are some shade of red: carmine, magenta, vermillion, scarlet, maroon. The purpose of red flowers seems to be two-fold. First, red makes a bright, obvious signal to the bird; and second, bees and butterflies can't see red, so they tend to ignore red flowers. These insects aren't very well suited to pollinate most hummingbird flowers, anyway, so their visits might not result in pollination. Some of the flowers, like the two penstemons, have turned-back petals, which makes it hard for bees and butterflies to gain a foothold on the flower. Hummingbirds can hover, thus don't need footholds.

Migration is another important dimension of bird niches. Insect-eating birds often migrate out of the area in the winter, when insect populations are at their lowest ebb, then migrate back in the spring when warmer temperatures mean that insects will be available once again.

Snakes at Chiricahua National Monument don't migrate during the winter, of course—they hibernate. Winter inactivity is one dimension of snake niches. Periodicity is another dimension; some snakes are active at night, some during the day. Different species occupy different habitats. A few live in leaf litter, like the Sonoran mountain kingsnake, others in rock piles, like the banded rock rattler. Some, like the Sonoran lyre snake, are good climbers and ascend tree trunks and branches in search of prey, mostly lizards and small mammals. Another tree climber, the Sonoran whipsnake, or Sonoran racer, feeds on young birds and arboreal lizards. Other species are aquatic or semiaquatic; in the monument, several different species of garter snakes thrive in and around streambed pools, where they feed on frogs, toads, and tadpoles. So thoroughly have snakes exploited all possible niches that there is even one—the Sonoran blind snake—that burrows in loose soil and feeds on ants, termites, and ant larvae. Since it spends so much time underground, it has little need for eyesight, and its eyes are vestigial organs.

Just as I expected, the gray-breasted jay returns to unearth and eat the cracker it buried an hour earlier. Ordinarily, the jay would be recovering acorns, not crackers. In fact, seed burial by jays is an important aspect of the oak niche.

Plants don't have niches in the same sense that animals do. Because the "food" of one plant—water, mineral nutrients, and sunshine—is much the same as the food of another plant, it is difficult to see how plants can partition the available food. Seed and seedling stages, however, do provide plants a chance to create distinct niches. The mission of a seed is to germinate and grow into a plant that will produce more seeds. Anything seeds require to foster this process is part of their niche.

Emory oak has a very precise seed niche. For a tree to produce a bumper crop of acorns in the fall, there must have been at least fifteen inches of rain during the preceding winter. Acorns drop from the tree in the autumn and germinate the following summer once the rains have come. At least ten inches of rainfall are needed to stimulate germination. Not only that, but the acorns will not germinate unless covered by soil. Here the niches of the gray-breasted jay and the Emory oak overlap, as the food-caching habits of the jay complement the germination requirements of the acorn.

Although plants may not partition food, they do partition certain other resources—pollinators, for example. Two species of columbine—the yellow and the red—grow in the monument. Yellow columbine is pollinated by hawkmoths, which are the only creatures with tongues long enough to reach the nectar in the bottom of the five elongated nectar tubes, or spurs. Red columbine, which has much shorter spurs, is pollinated largely by hummingbirds, which are attracted to the flowers by their red color. These two columbines create distinct niches for themselves by attracting different pollinators.

# THINGS THAT GO BUMP IN THE NIGHT: MORE NICHES

At dusk, I leave the campground and drive up the Bonita Canyon road to Massai Point. The last rays of sunshine on the cliffs are just now fading. A golden glow remains, probably from the yellow-green lichens that paint nearly every upright slab of rock in the monument.

As I drive around a bend, my headlights pick out a whitetail deer at the side of the road. The deer whips its head around, looks at me with dark eyes, snorts, then bounds into the dim forest. I glimpse its white hindquarters and upraised tail before it disappears.

Both mule and whitetail deer are common in the monument. The easiest way to tell them apart is by their tails. Whitetail deer raise their tails like flags when alarmed. Underneath, the tail is white; above, it is black or dark brown with a white border. The tail of a mule deer is creamy or tan with a black tip and is not raised when the deer is alarmed.

The mule deer occupies somewhat drier, brushier habitats than the whitetail deer and does not range so high in elevation. In the Chiricahua Mountains both species feed on a variety of shrubs, particularly the foliage of mountain mahogany, juniper, silk-tassel, Arizona oak, and Emory oak. They also eat juniper berries, sumac berries, and acorns. At elevations above the woodland, whitetail deer feed on white fir, Douglas-fir, netleaf oak, and Gambel oak.

By the time I park at Massai Point, the sun has set. A golden band of sky scallops the successive mountain ranges, now gray in the twilight. Crickets chirp softly. A last towhee calls from the underbrush.

Just as the lights of Willcox begin to appear beyond the Dos Cabezas Mountains, a bat flutters overhead. It has the characteristic flickering flight of the western pipistrelle, a small bat that commonly forages at dawn and dusk. The bat swings by my head, probably harvesting some of the mosquitoes I have attracted.

Bats depend little on sight to find their food; in fact, with some exceptions, their vision is poorly developed. Instead, they use echolocation, a kind of sonar. By emitting high-pitched squeaks (largely beyond the range of human hearing), they bounce sound waves off their prey, then interpret the returning sound waves to determine the size, location, and movement of their quarry.

Bats are selective about the kinds of insects they eat. Some, like the big brown bat, specialize on beetles, others, like the hoary bat, on moths. This kind of specialization enables them to partition their food resources. Larger bats tend to eat larger insects than smaller bats, another way of dividing up the available food. Bats in an area also partition foraging space. Slow-flying, highly maneuverable bats, such as the silver-haired bat, forage between, within, and below the tree canopy. They tend to select individual insects and consume them one time, often retiring to a perch to do so. Other slow-bats are terrestrial foragers with relatively well developed eyesight. They search for prey on the ground where vegetation is sparse, scouting six inches to three feet above the ground until they see something edible. Then they drop upon it, capture it, and retire to a feeding roost to eat it. The pallid bat is a good example of this group. Fast-flying bats, among them the long-legged myotis and Brazilian freetail, forage in open air, covering large distances each night. Because they feed only as they fly, they tend to eat smaller insects. The western pipistrelle is a filter feeder; it locates insect swarms and flies through them, mouth open, engulfing all the insects in its path.

Not all bats forage for insects. Some tropical bats specialize on fruit, fish, mice, reptiles, or birds. Some, such as the long-tongued bat and the long-nosed bat, depend

JAVELINA

on nectar and pollen. These bats visit night-blooming flowers—at Chiricahua National Monument, mainly the flowers of Palmer agave and Parry agave. In the Sonoran Desert, nectar-feeding bats visit flowers of saguaro, organ pipe, and senita, all columnar cacti that bloom late in the spring.

Back at the campground I settle into my sleeping bag inside the tent. From a nearby perch a whippoorwill sings persistently, reiterating its own name. The liquid notes pour over the quiet campground, then evaporate as the birds flies to a more distant perch. By foraging at night, whippoorwills avoid competition with the numerous insect-eating birds active by day.

Owls also exploit the niches that open when darkness arrives. They specialize on the vast number of nocturnal rodents, reptiles, and insects, leaving diurnal animals to hawks and eagles. Owls are able to find food at night by using both sight and sound. Their vision is specialized to work well in what we consider complete darkness, and asymmetrically placed ears enable them to pinpoint the exact source of a sound.

As the whippoorwill's voice fades into the distance, I drop off to sleep. A scuttering among the shrubs startles me awake. Against my will, my heart pounds; city-bred habits of wariness die hard. Straining my ears, I listen for the noise that awakened me and hear shuffling and bumping. Skunks, I suppose, probably foraging in the leaf litter or under branches for beetles, small rodents, eggs, nuts, berries, or even carrion or garbage.

Southeastern Arizona and southwestern New Mexico is the only region in the United States where four species of skunks—the striped, spotted, hooded, and hognosed—can be found together. All four occur at Chiricahua National Monument, the most common being the striped.

Striped and spotted skunks can be very bold. George Olin, in his book on southwestern mammals, tells how one strolled into his tent and tugged on the hair of a sleeping camper. The best policy is to let them roam un-hindered—or to keep your tent zipped shut. The conspicuous white markings, visible even on a dark night, make it easy for hunting animals to recognize and avoid the skunk. This works out well for all concerned, since the skunk apparently doesn't like its scent any better than the rest of us and prefers not to spray unless it's absolutely necessary. Great horned owls prey upon skunks occasionally, but on the whole, skunks have few natural enemies other than humans.

The shuffling and bumping sounds approach my tent. Too much noise for a skunk, I decide. I shine my flashlight out the tent, but the mosquito netting scatters the beam. It's like trying to peer through fog. Slowly, quietly, I unzip the tent and poke my head outside. The beam shines on a red eye some twenty feet away. Then I see the coarse, brown fur, spindly legs, and massive head of a javelina. It snuffles at the ground—looking for acorns, perhaps, or garbage. Every so often it makes a whumping sound, as through expelling air through its nostrils.

I watch for a while, then retire to bed once more, leaving the night to its true owners.

---

The smallest owl in North America—the elf owl—is migratory. Elf owls arrive in the Chiricahua Mountains in late March or early April and nest in tree cavities, typically in sycamores. (In the Sonoran Desert, elf owls nest in holes in the giant saguaro cacti.) They forage throughout the night, mainly for moths and crickets in the spring and beetles in the summer. Their strictly nocturnal habits mean that, once the weather turns cold, they must migrate far to the south, where insects remain active at night during the winter.

The western screech owl and the whiskered screech owl are year-round residents at the monument. Where they occur together, the whiskered takes the denser woods, leaving more open woodland to the western.

Both feed on crickets, grasshoppers, spiders, centipedes, beetles, scorpions, and other small creatures; however, the western screech owl likes to perch on the outer limb of a tree and swoop down upon its prey, while the whiskered screech owl prefers to glean insects from the limbs and leaves of trees.

The northern pygmy owl, also a year-round resident at the monument, has departed from the typical owl niche by becoming diurnal. It feeds during the early morning and late afternoon hours on small animals such as songbirds, chipmunks, and mice. In fact, songbirds mob roosting pygmy owls, and if you can successfully imitate the call of a pygmy owl, you'll find yourself surrounded by dozens of agitated, twittering birds.

---

# AN OVERFLOWING NOTEBOOK: SPECIES DIVERSITY AT CHIRICAHUA NATIONAL MONUMENT

Starting in North Bonita Canyon, the Natural Bridge Trail follows the canyon bottom through pine-oak woodland where pine siskins sizzle like bacon in the treetops and rufous-sided towhees proclaim "dirt-whee" from hidden perches. A flock of gray-breasted jays proceeds noisily ahead of me, leaving bouncing branches in their wake.

Gray-breasted jays are permanent residents of the pine-oak woodland and oak woodland, where their distinctive "wheat, wheat" call and clopping wings can be heard throughout the day.

Many birds try to be as inconspicuous as possible. When spotted, they interpose a trunk or a branch between themselves and the viewer, or they fly to the protection of a distant tree. The gray-breasted jay however, is anything but shy. In campgrounds, these birds quickly become habituated to people, and whenever I set up camp in the monument's campground, they soon arrive to beg for handouts or to make sardonic comments on my tent-erecting abilities. Nor are they shy in their relations with other species. If two birds squabble in the tree tops, a gray-breasted jay, if not already at the center of the fracas, is likely to investigate it.

Using their strong bills, gray-breasted jays pry under twigs and stones or sweep aside layers of leaf litter to find acorns, juniper berries, beetles, and other insects. Usually they search for food on the ground, but occasionally they catch flying insects on the wing and work tree canopies for acorns and insects. Like other jays, gray-breasted jays commonly store food items in holes in the ground, using a leaf, a bit of bark, or a stone as a lid.

When I see one gray-breasted jay, I know I'll see others before too long, because they travel in flocks of eight to twenty. Typically, a flock contains two or three mated pairs, several unmated adults, and a variable number of yearlings, which have not yet attained breeding age. All members of a flock, except for rare immigrants, are related. They are like extended families of grandparents, parents, children, and unattached aunts and uncles. The flock holds a common territory and defends it against all interlopers.

Gray-breasted jays are communal breeders; the birds in a flock cooperate in building nests, finding food, and feeding nestlings and fledglings. Because the entire flock concentrates its efforts on one or two sets of nestlings, gray-breasted jays are phenomenally successful at raising young. An average of seventy-two percent of their nestlings survive to adulthood, compared to an average of fifty percent for songbirds that are not communal breeders.

Soon I leave the gray-breasted jays and the woodland behind as the trail climbs out of the canyon. Striding through the chaparral on the ridgetop, I notice few birds—a flock of shy and nervous chipping sparrows, a blue-gray gnatcatcher flicking its tail and wheezing, a complaining rufous-sided towhee. From distant cliffs a canyon wren mocks. As soon as the trail drops into Picket Canyon, however, birdsong fills the air as though someone had turned up the volume on a stereo. In the medley of notes I can pick out the voices of a black-headed grosbeak, two Scott's orioles, and several gray-breasted jays.

Walking through the canyon-bottom woodland, I stop to watch a pair of black-throated gray warblers in a pinyon. They whisper "tsip, tsip" to one another as they glean insects from the needles. A bridled titmouse scolds me as I pass under an Arizona oak. From some distance away, a mourning dove's lullaby floats through the trees.

Apache pines grow in magnificent stands in the bottom of Picket Canyon, along with Chihuahua pine and various oaks. This is good squirrel habitat, or so I judge from the evidence on the ground: fibrous cores of pine cones stripped of scales. Suddenly a gray squirrel with a rust-colored belly dashes up the trunk of a nearby juniper and proceeds to the upper branches of an Apache pine. Its red underparts and the absence of tufts on its ears help me distinguish this Apache fox squirrel from other southwestern tree squirrels. The Chiricahua Mountains are the only place in the United States where the Apache fox squirrel occurs. In Mexico, it can be found far south into the Sierra Madre.

The squirrel crouches on the branch and turns a pine cone rapidly between its front paws as though it were eating corn on the cob. Pine scales fall like raindrops. In addition to pine seeds, Apache fox squirrels also eat acorns, walnuts, and juniper berries. They supplement their seed diet with occasional fungi and insects, and, during the breeding season, with flower parts. Unlike some squirrels, Apache fox squirrels seldom cache food; since their woodland habitat remains relatively free of snow in the winter, they can forage year-round.

APACHE FOX SQUIRREL

A lichen is a symbiotic association of an alga and a fungus. Symbiotic associations are mutually beneficial for both organisms. In this case, the alga provides food for the fungus, and the fungus provides water and protection from desiccation for the alga. The bulk of every lichen is transparent fungal tissue; the algal layer just under the surface gives it color.

By producing weak acids, lichens dissolve bare rock. Rootlike tubes called hyphae then penetrate an inch or so into the rock and absorb the nutrients necessary for growth. Hyphae also cause mechanical damage to rock by swelling when wet and contracting when dry. Digestion of rocks by lichens is the first step in soil formation.

Lichens grow where it is too hot or too infertile or too dry or too shady for other plants: boulders, cliff faces, rock rubble, tree trunks, fallen logs. Crustose lichens are flat and scalelike and can hardly be pried away from their substrate, usually rocks. Foliose and fruticose lichens may be leafy, hairlike, fingerlike, or strap-shaped and can grow on trees and logs as well as rocks. The vivid chartreuse lichen on cliffs and rocks throughout the monument is a crustose species.

Many trees in the monument, especially in canyon bottoms, support a miniature forest of foliose and fruticose lichens on their trunks and branches. Thirty different species have been collected on silver-leaf oak alone, twenty on alligator juniper. These lichens are not parasites on the tree; they simply occupy it for living space, just as the tree itself occupies a particular plot of ground. On any tree, the lichens are distributed according to their requirements for moisture, light, and nutrition. Some need the brighter light of the canopy, others prefer the shady trunk. A few grow only on particular kinds of trees, just on Douglas-fir or silver-leaf oak, for example.

The trail ends on a bouldery hillside where a small sign points to the natural bridge across the canyon. It takes me a few minutes to distinguish the rock arch from the stacked and broken boulders. Garlands of pinyons and oaks festoon the cliffs. Magnesium has painted black streaks where water streams down rock walls after storms. And, as everywhere in the monument, yellow-green lichens spatter the rocks.

Riffling through the pages of my notebook, I'm surprised to see how many different plants and animals I've noted along this short trail. If I had recorded every species I'd observed, my notebook would be overflowing.

Chiricahua National Monument lies within one of the most biologically diverse regions north of the Mexican border. Nearly 700 different species of flowering plants and ferns have been collected within the monument's boundaries. Adding mosses, lichens, liverworts, and algae to the plant list would bring the total even higher. One hundred sixty-nine bird species are known from the monument; of these 108 are permanent or summer residents. Seventy species of mammals, thirty-two of snakes, sixteen of lizards, nine of frogs and toads, and one of turtle complete the catalogue of the monument's higher animals. And of course there is a multitude of insects, spiders, and other multi-legged creatures that have not been cataloged.

As I munch on an apple, I watch a white-breasted nuthatch creep around and around the branch of an Emory oak, searching for insects, no doubt. It occurs to me that I could fill my notebook with the names of all the species found over the course of a year on just one Emory oak. Certain butterflies lay their eggs on oak leaves, and their caterpillars eat the developing leaves. Leaf mining insects occupy the tissue just below the upper surface, and the larvae of certain wasps live in galls on the underside. In addition, many insects shelter among the leaves in the daytime or during storms. When I consider the trunk and all the possible positions for insects within, underneath, and on top of the bark, I realize that a staggering number of insects can occupy a single tree. Most of these insects are fair game for larger predators—birds, squirrels, and bats—and I would have to add their names to my list of the Emory oak's inhabitants, too. That same Emory oak might play host to several species of nesting birds. Bridled titmice nest in cavities in the trunk, as do screech owls, ash-throated flycatchers, and many others. Other birds, such as the gray-breasted jay, nest in the canopy once it is fully leafed out. The Emory oak even provides habitat for plants—parasitic mistletoes on the branches and dainty lichens on the trunk.

The number of habitats within an Emory oak community is not limited to the individual oaks. Between the oaks sunloving wildflowers, grasses, and shrubs grow, and each of these has its complement of insect and animal users. The lark sparrow, for example, nests in grassy spots among the oaks. Ants nest on bare ground between grass clumps and collect the fallen seeds of grasses and wildflowers. Lizards feed on the ants. Several species of hummingbirds sip nectar at the flowers of red penstemon that grow in woodland openings. Carnivores such as bobcats and coyotes prowl through the woodland in search of lizards, birds, and other prey.

Seeing how complex is the web of niches in an apparently simple community, I can imagine the ramifications of adding other tree species. If I add Chihuahua pine to the oaks, I supply foraging habitat for the Grace's warbler and pygmy nuthatch. If I add Schott's yucca, I provide a nesting site for the Scott's oriole. The more complex the mosaic of biotic communities in an area, the greater opportunities for niche differentiation and the larger the number of species that can coexist.

I can account for animal species diversity—in part, at least—by referring to plants. But how can I account for plant species diversity? One reason for the large number of plant species in the monument is the variety of habitats: scree slopes, boulder piles, cliffs, ridges, shaded banks, canyon bottoms, streambeds, springs, and so forth. Moreover, this array of habitats interacts with the various microclimates to create even more places for plants to live. A cliff that faces south is not the same habitat as one that faces north, for example, nor will a broad canyon bottom support the same plant species as a narrow one.

Another factor that boosts plant diversity here is the biseasonal rainfall. Winter rains promote one distinctive set of wildflowers in the spring, summer rains an entirely different set. Changing climatic patterns over the past 10,000 years have also augmented plant diversity. As the regional climate changed from cool and wet to warm and semiarid, many plant species died out locally, but others migrated into southeastern Arizona from different biotic regions. The diversity of habitats in the monument provided living space for these migrants.

In the upper branches of a nearby Apache pine a pair of hepatic tanagers, the male the color of a mango, the female the color of a ripening pear, slips quietly in and out of the drooping needles. Hepatic tanagers occur far south into the Sierra Madre and reach their northern limit of distribution in the Southwest. In the Sierra Madre, a region of extensive pine and oak forests, most of the moisture comes as summer thunderstorms. Madrean species such as the hepatic tanager find a counterpart to this climate and vegetation in the oak woodlands and pine forests of southeastern Arizona. The numerous Madrean species in Chiricahua National Monument include the Emory oak, Apache pine, Mexican chickadee, olive warbler, and Mexican garter snake. The coatimundi and the magnificent hummingbird have come from even farther south—the tropics of Mexico and Central America.

**WOODRAT**

Other regions have also contributed to the flora and fauna, and thus the diversity, of the monument. The lark bunting and plains harvest mouse are some typical Great Plains species that reach the grasslands of southeastern Arizona. The Sonoran Desert to the west and the Chihuahuan Desert to the east have contributed many species, too, among them the cactus wren, black-throated sparrow, desert pocket mouse, Merriam's kangaroo rat, and Sonoran lyre snake. The desert influence, like that of the Great Plains, is most noticeable in grasslands and shrublands at the base of the Chiricahua Mountains.

The contribution of the Rocky Mountains has been small. Such plants as Gambel oak, buckbrush, and New Mexico locust and such animals as Williamson's sapsucker and Townsend's solitaire are typical of the Rocky Mountain region. Not surprisingly, the influence of the Rockies is greatest at the highest elevations, where, among the firs and spruces of the forest zone, ruby-crowned kinglets and red-breasted nuthatches find habitats similar to those they would occupy farther north in the mountains of Colorado and Wyoming.

# BEAR SIGN: PRESERVING SPECIES DIVERSITY

I notice bear scat on the trail as I head back the way I came. It's old and crumbly with manzanita seeds. My chances of seeing an actual bear today are slim. In fact, the probability that I'll see any of the larger carnivores that inhabit the region—the mountain lions, bobcats, coyotes, and gray foxes—is not high.

These animals are quite wary of humans, and rightly so. On the other hand, all of them are spotted regularly in the monument, and if I'm in the right place at the right time, I too might see a bear lumbering across the road or a mountain lion staring from atop a boulder. It's more likely that, as now, I'll see their signs: the conspicuous, gray droppings of coyotes, rocks overturned by bears looking for grubs, large paw prints in damp earth where a mountain lion drank at a streambed pool, the leaf-covered prey of a bobcat.

As people spread across the landscape of southeastern Arizona, destroying ever more grassland, woodland, and forest, large carnivores will become continually rarer as their habitat shrinks. Parks and monuments serve as refuges for these animals, but unfortunately the refuges provide enough territory for only a few individuals. Mountain lions, for example, cover up to two hundred square miles of hunting territory in a year, an area more than ten times that of Chiricahua National Monument.

Whenever I see a bear, a bobcat, or a gray fox, I count it as one of the luckiest days of my life, for it may be a sight my great-grandchildren will never see. Even now, only a few people—mostly old-timers—remember hearing the deep howl of the gray wolf in Arizona. At one time this beautiful animal was widespread in the West, but due to relentless hunting, it is now extirpated over much of its former range and may be on the verge of extinction. Jaguars, ocelots, and jagarundis, wild cats that once inhabited wooded terrain in southeastern Arizona, are rarely seen in the state anymore. Their numbers, too, have decreased dramatically because of hunting pressure and diminished habitat.

Henry David Thoreau once wrote of Concord that he was reading the landscape after his ancestors had torn out many of its pages. Here in the Southwest, also, many pages have been ripped from the book. I am thankful that national parks and monuments serve as reservoirs of species diversity. And I am hopeful that in another twenty years I will be able to walk this trail once again and watch an Apache fox squirrel harvest pine seeds, hear the conversational song of a black-headed grosbeak, see hummingbirds stab into the blossoms of Indian paintbrush, listen to cliff chipmunks bark 160 times a minute, and maybe even be startled by a bear.

HEART OF ROCKS WITH COCHISE HEAD IN THE BACKGROUND

CHIRICAHUA NATIONAL MONUMENT

SKUNKBUSH IN SILVER SPUR MEADOW

BIG TOOTH MAPLES IN PINERY CANYON

CHIRICAHUA NATIONAL MONUMENT

CHIRICAHUA NATIONAL MONUMENT

SCHOTTS YUCCA AND SILVERLEAF OAK IN BONITA CANYON

# THE PEOPLE

# LOOKING INTO THE PAST

The graveyard at the mouth of Bonita Canyon is a tiny one: two plots, each encircled by a wrought iron fence, and five graves. Wildflowers, weeds, and an alligator juniper provide all the decoration needed. Rocky hills behind the cemetery overlook the wide mouth of Bonita Canyon and the wavering line of sycamores, oaks, and ashes along the streambed. A gentle breeze stirs the branches of the juniper, and its shadows shiver on the headstone of Louis Prue.

One of the first settlers near Bonita Canyon, Prue was also the first to occupy this cemetery. In 1892 he died in a fall from a horse, and his neighbors buried him, as he had wished, at the mouth of Bonita Canyon so that he could see his cattle passing on their way to water.

Some of his neighbors are buried here, too: Neil Erickson, who "served five years in the army during the Indian wars," according to the plaque on the fence; his wife Emma Sophia, who remained undaunted by the "perils of Indian warfare, incessant toil and loneliness of a pioneer land;" and Hildegard and Ben, two of Neil and Emma's three children.

We call these valiant people pioneers, and indeed they were. But long before the first white-skinned pioneers occupied Bonita Canyon, Native American pioneers had arrived on the scene and made the land their own.

# THE EARLIEST SETTLERS

The little we know about the Native Americans who lived here between 8000 B.C. and the time of Christ comes from their artifacts—scattered accumulations of worked stone and pieces of pottery. Archeologists call these people Archaic Cochise after the remains of their camps, first described from Cochise County, Arizona.

They were seminomadic hunters and gatherers who no doubt made a good living from the land. Acorns, juniper berries, manzanita berries, grass seeds, pine nuts, and many more wild fruits and seeds were seasonally abundant. They would have supplemented their diet with meat—deer, rabbits, squirrels, quail. Most likely these Indians occupied the canyons of the Chiricahua Mountains temporarily as they harvested acorns, hunted game, or quarried rocks for arrowheads and other tools.

The Archaic way of life eventually gave rise to a sedentary, agricultural culture now known as the Mogollon. Mogollon people occupied much of western New Mexico and eastern Arizona below the Mogollon Rim. By about 2000 B.C., they were growing corn, beans, and squash. By about 500 B.C., they were living in rudimentary pithouses. They learned how to make pottery, how to farm the steep slopes and canyon bottoms of southwestern mountain ranges, and how to divert stream water to their tiny fields. They didn't entirely abandon their hunting and gathering past, however, and they continued to depend heavily on wild animals and gathered foods. Between A.D. 900 and 1100, the Anasazi culture to the north swamped Mogollon culture, and it lost its distinct identity. These peoples left the region entirely by A.D. 1450, part of the general, mysterious exodus of native tribes from their southwestern homelands.

# EXPANSION AND CONQUEST: THE APACHE ERA

After the Mogollon culture died out but before Anglo-Americans arrived on the scene, Apache Indians arrived in the Southwest. No one knows exactly when they came; when Coronado passed through southern Arizona in 1540, he found them already on the scene. A nomadic people, they lived primarily by hunting and gathering wild foods. By 1854, when southeastern Arizona was opened to homesteaders by the Gadsden Purchase, the Chiricahua Apaches had made the Chiricahua Mountains their homeland and stronghold.

Once they obtained horses from the early Spanish explorers and missionaries, the Apaches became a force to be reckoned with. They conducted raids upon Spanish settlements and Mexican Indians, taking horses and cattle. The situation worsened when American homesteaders began settling in the region. Most Americans showed little understanding or sympathy with the Apache way of life, regarding the Indians, for the most part, as less-than-human savages. While moderate Anglos argued that the Apaches could best be handled by settling them on reservations and teaching them to live by farming and hunting, others believed that the only way to control the Apaches was to exterminate the entire tribe. Bloody encounters between Apaches and Anglos became a feature of frontier life throughout the latter part of the nineteenth century.

The story of these raids and counter-raids, massacres and murders, reflects little credit on either side. In southeastern Arizona, the specific incident that triggered much of the bloodshed centered on Apache Pass, a narrow valley between the Dos Cabezas and Chiricahua mountains. The pass had been a reliable watering place for Apaches and occasional white travelers for many years. In 1858, the Butterfield Overland Mail began to use the pass on a regular basis and built a stage station there. Under the leadership of Cochise, the Chiricahua Apache had been fairly peaceable towards whites until, in 1861, Cochise was wrongfully accused of kidnapping a white boy. The U.S. military retaliated by capturing six Apache men, including three close relatives of Cochise, and hanging them at the stage station. Understandably infuriated, Cochise made it all but impossible for travelers to use the Apache Pass route for several years. Only after the establishment of Fort Bowie in 1862, at the cost of considerable loss of life, was a military escort available for travelers in the region.

Despite the existence of the fort, Cochise and his warriors attacked settlers in southeastern Arizona until 1872, when Colonel O. O. Howard, with the help of Thomas J. Jeffords, an army scout, achieved a peace with Cochise. The Apache leader and his tribe were settled on a reservation in the Sulphur Springs Valley, then were moved to Pinery Canyon in the Chiricahua Mountains. After Cochise died in 1874, the Chiricahua Apaches were moved from their homeland to the San Carlos Apache Reservation some distance to the north.

Not all of the Chiricahua Apache were content to be summarily exiled, and a group under the leadership of Natchez, a son of Cochise, broke from the reservation in 1880 and hid out in the rugged Sierra Madre in northern Mexico. The notorious Geronimo was part of this band. The Apaches began their campaigns against Anglo settlers all over again, and, predictably, white vigilantes retaliated.

Finally, in 1882, General George Crook, well known as an Indian fighter, was ordered to Arizona to take the problem in hand. He had a reputation for using friendly Apache scouts to hunt down hostile Apaches. "The only hope of success," he wrote, "lies in using their own methods—Apache vs. Apache." In 1883, with a force of 193 Apache scouts and one troop of cavalry, he invaded the Chiricahua Apache's stronghold in the Sierra Madre. Within a few months, Geronimo and the others returned to the San Carlos Reservation. Not for long, though. In May 1885 Geronimo and a group of followers bolted from the reservation again.

A few months earlier, the Tenth Cavalry, which had been stationed at Fort Davis near El Paso, had been ordered into the Arizona Territory. In April 1885 these buffalo soldiers were on their way, marching beside the newly laid tracks of the Southern Pacific Railroad. Once they arrived in Arizona, the thirty-eight officers and 696 enlisted men were distributed among several posts, including Fort Grant, some thirty miles south of the San Carlos Reservation. They were on the spot, then, when Geronimo and other experienced fighters—Natchez, Chihuahua, Mangus, and Old Nana—escaped in May.

The first troop—Troop E—of buffalo soldiers arrived in Bonita Canyon in late September 1885. It seems likely that they had been ordered there in reponse to a report of Apaches in the area. In November Troop H arrived and Troop E returned to Fort Grant. In January 1886, Troop E joined Troop H in Bonita Canyon and stayed until April of that year, when Troop I replaced them both. In all, buffalo soldiers occupied the camp at Bonita Canyon for nearly a year.

General Crook's intent in the Geronimo Campaign of 1885 and 1886 was to rely upon Apache scouts to track hostile Apaches in Mexico. In the meantime, he secured trails and waterholes along the border with buffalo soldiers. According to Crook, troops guarded every trail and waterhole from the Patagonia Mountains in southern Santa Cruz County, Arizona, to the Rio Grande in Texas.

For the buffalo soldiers, who were accustomed to guerilla warfare in the Texas desert, this waterhole campaign was hardly glamorous duty. Troops E and H saw some action when they first arrived in Bonita Canyon. A band of Apaches had raided a ranch in Whitetail Canyon at the northern end of the Chiricahua Mountains. The soldiers pursued the Apaches but did not catch up with them. Other than this brief flurry of activity, the buffalo soldiers at Bonita Canyon did little but act as couriers for the mail service from Fort Bowie to Cloverdale, New Mexico, mount an occasional patrol, and guard the waterhole.

Not much is known about the daily life in the buffalo soldiers' camp. Cavalry soldiers were issued clothing and gear, including a Springfield rifle, Colt revolver, gun sling, cartridge belt, tin cup, flatware, canteen, ammunition, tent, and two blankets. Soldiers replaced lost or ruined gear at their own expense. Standard army fare in those days was hardtack, bacon and coffee. In addition, the Bonita Canyon soldiers ate fresh beef supplied by Louis Prue and fresh fruit and vegetables provided by a homesteader named J. Hughes Stafford, who lived nearby.

The only traces of the buffalo soldiers in Bonita Canyon today are scattered bits of clothing and equipment—belt buckles, buttons, bottles, barrel hoops—and the chimney of the Faraway Ranch house. The large stone blocks of the chimney are carved with the names and troop designations of some sixty soldiers. Originally each of these stones was part of a freestanding monument constructed in honor of President James A. Garfield, who was assassinated by a crazed job-seeker in 1881. In the Civil War Garfield had commanded black troops, and as president he had been sympathetic to the problems of blacks in the post-slavery era. The largest stone in the monument bore an inscription in his memory.

While the buffalo soldiers of the Tenth Cavalry guarded the waterhole in Bonita Canyon, the Apache wars continued across the border. Eventually, General Crook, whose strategy for bringing the Apaches to heel

The Tenth Cavalry was one of six regiments of black troops created at the end of the Civil War. Four of the new black units were assigned to the infantry; the other two were horse soldiers, and became the Ninth and Tenth Regiments of the U.S. Cavalry. Formation of black troops served two purposes at that point in United States history. They reinforced the ranks of the army, which had been decimated by the Civil War, and they provided employment for at least a segment of the large, newly freed black population. By law, the officers of these black regiments were white.

From the start, the Tenth Cavalry served in Indian wars, first against the Cheyenne, Arapaho, and other tribes of the Great Plains, then in western Texas against Apaches and miscellaneous bandits, horse thieves, and bootleggers. It is uncomfortable today for us to contemplate a government of white men pitting black men against other men of color. There may have been more than a slight element of racism in sending black troops to fight guerilla wars in which loss of life was bound to be great. In any case, the men of the Tenth Cavalry quickly became seasoned fighters and earned the admiration and respect of their Indian foes, who called them "buffalo soldiers," perhaps because their curly, black hair was like that on a buffalo's head, or perhaps because they wore robes of buffalo skin during the cold winters on the Great Plains. They accepted the name proudly, and it is commonly used today to refer to all the black regiments of that era.

met with increasing criticism and little visible success, was forced to resign in favor of Brigadier General Nelson A. Miles early in 1886.

Miles had the peaceful Chiricahua Apaches in the area rounded up, marched to Holbrook 200 miles north, and sent to Florida by train. About the same time, he sent Lieutenant Charles B. Gatewood, a protege of Crook and the only officer on his staff whom Geronimo trusted, into Mexico for a parley with the Apache leader. Once Geronimo learned that Apache families had already been shipped to Florida, he capitulated. On September 3, 1886, an exhausted Geronimo and the remainder of his warriors surrendered to General Miles at Skeleton Canyon on the New Mexico border. Twelve days later, the camp at Bonita Canyon was abandoned for good.

This wasn't the end of Apaches in the Chiricahua Mountains, however. Although Geronimo and many other Apaches were dispatched to Florida by train, some escaped the general roundup. One of them, Big Foot Massai, passed through Bonita Canyon in 1892 and stole a horse from one of the ranchers. His pursuers lost his trail at the place now called Massai Point.

# PRESERVATION AND PROFIT: THE FARAWAY RANCH ERA

The three dormer windows of the Faraway Ranch house overlook a large clearing cut out of the oaks and junipers. Virginia creeper spills over the wire fence and clutches the stiffly hinged gate. A few venerable fruit trees grow among the weeds; they survive even though it has been many years since any human hand has watered them. As I walk across the yard, stickers hop from the ground to my socks as if magnetized. Behind the house, sweetpeas flower in profusion in a shaded planter, oblivious to neglect. The old stone chimney, built of blocks of different sizes, reminds me of the buffalo soldiers who, over one hundred years ago, camped in Bonita Canyon.

A short distance away, I find another relic of those days—a log cabin with a stone chimney and shingled roof. A lizard scutters across the porch as I step up to peer in the windows. This is the old Stafford cabin where J. Hughes Stafford and his child bride Pauline lived when they arrived in Bonita Canyon around 1879. The story is that Stafford, a Civil War veteran then in his forties, had passed through Salt Lake City on his way west. Thirteen-year-old Pauline had fallen in love with him and stowed away in his wagon. They married en route to Arizona, built a log cabin along Bonita Creek, and supported themselves and their several children by selling the fruit and vegetables from their orchard and garden to other settlers in the Sulphur Springs Valley and to the soldiers at Fort Bowie. Their cabin, remnants of their orchard, and the grave of their first child, Reveley Stafford, still remain.

Stafford's talk about his beautiful establishment in Bonita Canyon impressed one Emma Sophia Peterson, a Swedish immigrant then living in Fort Bowie, and she paid him a visit. She liked the canyon so much, according to the story, she decided to buy an unoccupied cabin near his place. This cabin, owned by Stafford, had been the officers' headquarters during the encampment of buffalo soldiers in Bonita Canyon. After Emma's marriage to Neil Erickson, another Swedish immigrant, the newlyweds filed homestead papers on the cabin and 160 acres of land around it, and in the summer of 1888, Emma, Neil, and their first child, Lillian, then five months old, moved to Bonita Canyon. Eventually Neil and Emma added two more children to their family: a son, Ben, in 1891, and another daughter, Hildegard, in 1895.

Neil Erickson, a resourceful, enterprising, hardworking man, had emigrated to the United States in 1879 at the age of twenty. Shortly after his arrival, he enlisted with the military and fought in the Fourth U.S. Cavalry against Apaches, primarily in New Mexico. During his tour of duty from 1881 to 1886 he advanced to the rank of first sergeant.

Emma, who was born in 1854, was remembered by her children as valiant, hard-working, and brave. Her first recorded action upon taking up residence in Bonita Canyon was to scrub the board floors and wash the doors and windows of their new home. In fact, so thoroughly did she clean, the floors were still damp at bedtime, and the three of them—Neil, Emma, and baby Lillian—slept under the stars that first night, Neil with a gun by his side in case of Indian raids.

When the Ericksons moved into the former officers' quarters, it was a two-room cabin. A skilled carpenter, Neil soon added a third room and a stone storehouse that was meant to serve double duty as shelter from Indian attacks. With the exception of one brief scare when Massai came through the area and made off with some of Stafford's horses, the shelter proved most useful as a storehouse. Neil and Emma remodeled the house several times around the turn of the century, adding another story and several outbuildings. They built fences, installed a windmill, planted a fruit orchard and vegetable garden, raised crops for cattle and horses, and kept pigs, chickens, and turkeys. Bit by bit, the original homestead turned into a hard-working ranch.

In 1903, Neil became a ranger for the U.S. Forest Service. By 1917, he was promoted to district ranger and posted to the Dragoon and Whetstone mountains. Eventually Neil was transferred to Walnut Canyon National Monument in northern Arizona, and he and Emma lived there until his retirement in 1927. In the absence of Neil and Emma, management of the ranch fell to the children, particularly Lillian, the oldest.

Lillian and Hildegard bought the old Stafford homestead, thus enlarging their holdings to include most of lower Bonita Canyon. They named their expanded establishment Faraway Ranch. At this time, the ranch was a working cattle ranch. Cattle prices were so low, however, that many ranchers had started to take in paying guests. Lillian and Hildegard decided to do the same. Hildegard, a friendly, exuberant woman, often had friends to stay overnight at the ranch anyway, and accommodating paying guests was simply an extension of her natural hospitality. And because Lillian had always been interested in cattle and horses, the idea of a dude ranch appealed to her, too.

In just a few years, the burden of operating the ranch fell entirely to Lillian as Hildegard married and moved to California, and Ben took up ranching in nearby Whitetail Canyon. It was up to Lillian, then, to pay off the debt on the Stafford place and keep Faraway Ranch in order. She later wrote that even though carrying on seemed an impossibility at times, she never thought of deserting. "There seemed," she said, "nothing else to do but stick or die."

In 1923, Lillian married Edward Riggs, the son of a local ranching family whose holdings nearly surrounded Faraway Ranch. Although it is said that Lillian and Ed had been childhood sweethearts, the marriage also has aspects of a merger between rival corporations. In any case, it endured until Ed's death from a stroke in 1950.

As a child, Ed had been fascinated by glimpses of the rock formations in Rhyolite Canyon. Shortly after his marriage, he found an opportunity to explore them further. A party of hunters wounded a deer and pursued it up Rhyolite Canyon until they lost its trail. Hating to leave a wounded animal at large, Ed went back with Lillian to look for the deer the following day. After some distance, the canyon became impassable to horses, so they tied up their mounts and continued on foot. Lillian

flushed the deer, and they gave chase but lost its trail again. By then, however, they found themselves in rock formations so magnificent they forgot about their quarry. No doubt with an eye to potential profits, they decided to build a trail into the wonderland of rocks for their paying guests.

Recognizing the scenic value of the rock wonderland, Lillian and Ed began to lobby for its preservation in the National Park system. Altruism and love for the area inspired them in part, but they must also have hoped that a national monument in their backyard would boost business at the guest ranch. They showed photographs of the rock formations at county fairs and chambers of commerce, promoting the idea of a national park everywhere they could. Largely due to their efforts, Chiricahua National Monument was established in 1924. Ed Riggs served as trail foreman for the Civilian Conservation Corps crew that constructed the monument's buildings, roads, and trails.

Neil and Emma lived to see the transformation of the wilderness they had pioneered into a national monument. After her parents died, Neil in 1937, Emma in 1950, Lillian buried them in the little cemetery at the mouth of Bonita Canyon.

Following Ed's death in 1950, Lillian was back to managing the ranch on her own, undaunted by blindness. (At the age of thirty-five, she had fallen from a horse, and as a result had become blind nineteen years later.) As "the lady boss of Faraway Ranch," she was even featured in an article in the *Saturday Evening Post*. The ranch remained in business until Lillian retired to a rest home in nearby Willcox in 1975. After her death in 1977, the Park Service purchased Faraway Ranch and all its furnishings. The ranch, now part of the Faraway Ranch Historic District, was placed on the National Register of Historic Places on August 27, 1980.

Leaving the Stafford cabin, I stroll back toward the

ranch house. My foot strikes a piece of metal—an old lid rusted nearly black, the letters embossed on its upper surface impossible to decipher. I lay it back among the weeds. The people are gone but their objects endure. People always leave something behind—an arrowhead, a potsherd, a letter, a diary, an inscription, a contract, a cartridge casing, a photograph, a windmill, a peace treaty, a plum tree, an anecdote. Some things endure, and from these documents, relics, and memories, we piece together the story we call history.

The distant roar of a jet overhead pulls me from the past back into the present. Faraway Ranch is as far away as it ever was from the spirit of jet travel, traffic jams, double-bolted doors, and sirens in the night, and it is still just as close to the plants and animals that have woven around it a web of life and seasons and changes.

# FURTHER READING

## The Rocks

Enlows, H. E. 1955. Welded tuffs of Chiricahua National Monument, Arizona. *Bulletin of the Geological Society of America* 66: 1215–1246.

Fernandez, L. A., Jr., and H. E. Enlows. 1966. Petrography of the Faraway Ranch Formation, Chiricahua National Monument, Arizona. *Bulletin of the Geological Society of America* 77: 1017–1030.

Francis, P. 1983. Giant volcanic calderas. *Scientific American* 248 (June): 60–70.

Marjaniemi, D. K. 1970. *Geologic History of an Ash-flow Sequence and Its Source Area in the Basin and Range Province of Southeastern Arizona.* Ph.D. dissertation, University of Arizona, Tucson.

Sabins, F. F., Jr. 1957. Geology of the Cochise Head and western part of the Vanar quadrangles, Arizona. *Bulletin of the Geological Society of America* 68: 1315–1342.

## The Setting

Sellers, W. D., and R. H. Hill. 1974. *Arizona Climate.* Tucson: University of Arizona Press.

Shreve, F. 1915. *The Vegetation of a Desert Mountain Range as Conditioned by Climatic Factors.* Carnegie Institution of Washington Publication no. 217. Washington, D. C.

## The Plants and Animals

Balda, R. P. 1967. *Ecological Relationships of the Breeding-birds of the Chiricahua Mountains, Arizona.* Ph.D. dissertation, University of Illinois.

———. 1969. Foliage use by birds of the oak-juniper woodland and ponderosa pine forest in southeastern Arizona. *Condor* 71: 399–412.

———. 1970. Effects of spring leaf fall on composition and density of breeding birds in two southern Arizona woodlands. *Condor* 72: 325–331.

Black, H. L. 1974. A North Temperate bat community: Structure and prey populations. *Journal of Mammalogy* 55: 138–157.

Bowers, J. E. 1987. *100 Roadside Wildflowers of Southwest Woodlands.* Tucson: Southwest Parks and Monuments Association.

———, and S. P. McLaughlin. 1982. Plant species diversity in Arizona. *Madroño* 29: 227–233.

Brown, D. E. 1984. *Arizona's Tree Squirrels.* Phoenix: Arizona Game and Fish Department.

Brown, J. H., and A. Kodric-Brown. 1979. Convergence, competition, and mimicry in a temperate community of hummingbird-pollinated flowers. *Ecology* 60: 1022–1035.

Brown, J. L. 1963. Social organization and behavior of the Mexican jay. *Condor* 65: 126–153.

———. 1970. Comparative breeding and altruistic behavior in the Mexican jay, *Aphelocoma ultramarina. Animal Behavior* 18: 366–378.

———. 1974. Alternate routes to sociality in jays—With a theory for the evolution of altruism and communal breeding. *American Zoologist* 14: 63–80.

Darrow, R. A. 1950. The arboreal lichen flora of southeastern Arizona. *American Midland Naturalist* 43: 484–502.

Day, G. I. 1964. *An Investigation of White-tailed Deer (Odocoileus virginianus couesi) Forage Relationships in the Chiricahua Mountains.* M.S. thesis, University of Arizona, Tucson.

Dunford, C. 1974. Annual cycles of cliff chipmunks in the Santa Catalina Mountains, Arizona. *Journal of Mammalogy* 55: 401–416.

Gehlbach, F. R. 1981. *Mountain Islands and Desert Seas: A Natural History of the U.S.-Mexican Borderlands.* College Station: Texas A & M University Press.

Goldberg, S. R. 1971. Reproductive cycle of the ovoviviparous iguanid lizard *Sceloporus jarrovi* Cope. *Herpetologica* 27: 123–131.

Hale, M. E. 1983. *The Biology of Lichens,* 3rd ed. London: Edward Arnold.

Harlan, A. D. 1977. *Arctostaphylos Species in the Santa Catalina Mountains of Arizona.* Ph.D. dissertation, University of Arizona, Tucson.

Hoffmeister, D. F. 1986. *Mammals of Arizona.* Tucson: University of Arizona Press.

Howell, D. J. 1976. Plant-loving bats, bat-loving plants. *Natural History* 85 (Feb.): 52−59.

Hutchinson, G. E. 1959. Homage to Santa Rosalia, or why are there so many kinds of animals? *American Naturalist* 93: 145−159.

Kaufmann, J. H., D. V. Lanning, and S. E. Poole. 1976. Current status and distribution of the coati in the United States. *Journal of Mammalogy* 57: 621−637.

Ligon, J. D. 1968. *The Biology of the Elf Owl, Micrathene whitneyi.* Miscellaneous Publication of the Museum of Zoology no. 136. Ann Arbor: University of Michigan.

―――――, and R. P. Balda. 1968. Recent data on summer birds of the Chiricahua Mountains area, southeastern Arizona. *Transactions of the San Diego Society of Natural History* 15: 41−50.

MacRoberts, M. H. 1970. Notes on the food habits and food defense of the acorn woodpecker. *Condor* 72: 196−204.

Marshall, J. T. 1957. Birds of the pine-oak woodland in southern Arizona and adjacent Mexico. *Pacific Coast Avifauna* 32: 1−125.

Maza, B. G. 1965. *The Mammals of the Chiricahua Mountain Region, Cochise County, Arizona.* M.S. thesis, University of Arizona, Tucson.

Miller, R. B. 1985. Hawkmoth-pollination of *Aquilegia chrysantha* (Ranunculaceae) in southern Arizona. *Southwestern Naturalist* 30: 69−76.

National Geographic Book Service. 1983. *Field Guide to the Birds of North America.* Washington, D.C.: National Geographic Society.

Olin, G. 1961. *Mammals of the Southwest Mountains and Mesas.* Tucson: Southwest Parks and Monuments Assoc.

Pase, C. P. 1969. Survival of *Quercus turbinella* and *Q. emoryi* seedlings in an Arizona chaparral community. *Southwestern Naturalist* 14: 149−155.

Phillips, A., J. Marshall, and G. Monson. 1964. *The Birds of Arizona.* Tucson: University of Arizona Press.

Pulliam, H. R., and M. R. Brand. 1975. The production and utilization of seeds in plains grassland of southeastern Arizona. *Ecology* 56: 1158−1166.

Pyle, R. M. 1981. *The Audubon Society Field Guide to North American Butterflies.* New York: Alfred A. Knopf.

Rea, A. M. 1983. *Once a River: Bird Life and Habitat Changes on the Middle Gila.* Tucson: University of Arizona Press.

Reeves, T. 1976. *Vegetation and Flora of Chiricahua National Monument, Cochise County, Arizona.* M.S. thesis, Arizona State University, Tempe.

Ross, A. 1967. Ecological aspects of the food habits of insectivorous bats. *Proceedings of the Western Foundation of Vertebrate Zoology* 1: 204−263.

Simon, C. A. 1975. The influence of food abundance on territory size in the iguanid lizard *Sceloporus jarrovi.* *Ecology* 56: 993−998.

Stebbins, R. C. 1966. *A Field Guide to Western Reptiles and Amphibians.* Boston: Houghton Mifflin.

Steiner, A. L. 1975. Bedding and nesting material gathering in rock squirrels, *Spermophilus (Otospermophilus) variegatus grammurus* (Say) Sciuridae, in the Chiricahua Mountains of Arizona. *Southwestern Naturalist* 20: 363−369.

Tramontano, J. P. 1964. *Comparative Studies of the Rock Wren and the Canyon Wren.* M.S. thesis, University of Arizona, Tucson.

Weber, W. A. 1963. *Lichens of the Chiricahua Mountains, Arizona.* University of Colorado Studies, Series in Biology no. 10. Boulder: University of Colorado Press.

Westcott, P. W. 1969. Relationships among three species of jays wintering in southeastern Arizona. *Condor* 71: 353–359.

Whitaker, J. O., Jr. 1980. *The Audubon Society Field Guide to North American Mammals.* New York: Alfred A. Knopf.

**The People**

Baumler, M. F. 1984. *The Archeology of Faraway Ranch, Arizona: Prehistoric, Historic, and 20th Century.* Publications in Anthropology no. 24. Tucson: Western Archeological and Conservation Center, National Park Service.

Jackson, E. 1970. *The Natural History Story of Chiricahua National Monument.* Globe, AZ: Southwest Parks and Monuments Association.

Lister, R. H., and F. C. Lister. 1983. *Those Who Came Before.* Tucson: Southwest Parks and Monuments Association and University of Arizona Press.

Tagg, M. D. 1987. *The Camp at Bonita Canyon: A Buffalo Soldier Camp in Chiricahua National Monument, Arizona.* Publications in Anthropology no. 42. Tucson: Western Archeological and Conservation Center, National Park Service.

Terrell, J. W. 1972. *Apache Chronicle.* New York: World Publishing Company.

Torres, L., and M. Baumler. 1984. *Historic Structure Report, Historical and Archeological Data Sections: A History of the Building and Structures of Faraway Ranch, Chiricahua National Monument, Arizona.* Denver: Denver Service Center, National Park Service.

Janice Emily Bowers, a botanist with the U.S. Geological Survey, received her bachelor's degree in botany from the University of Arizona in 1976. Since then she has prepared floras of Organ Pipe Cactus National Monument and the Rincon Mountains. She is the author of *Seasons of the Wind: A Naturalist's Look at the Plant Life of Southwestern Sand Dunes* and *100 Roadside Wildflowers of Southwest Woodlands.* Her current interests include cats, quilts, biographies, and Greek tragedy.